Transportation and World Development

Transportation and World Development

Wilfred Owen

Hutchinson
London / Melbourne / Sydney / Auckland / Johannesburg

Hutchinson Education

An imprint of Century Hutchinson Ltd
62–65 Chandos Place, London WC2N 4NW

Century Hutchinson Australia Pty Ltd
PO Box 496, 16–22 Church Street, Hawthorn, Victoria 3122, Australia

Century Hutchinson New Zealand Limited
PO Box 40-086, Glenfield, Auckland 10, New Zealand

Century Hutchinson South Africa (Pty) Limited
PO Box 337, Bergvlei, 2012 South Africa

First published in Great Britain 1987

Part of chapter six originally appeared as "Transportation and World
Development" in *Transportation Quarterly* 39, no. 3 (July 1985).

The paper used in this book is acid-free.

ISBN 0 09 173175 5 (cased)
ISBN 0 09 173170 4 (paperback)

To E. B. O.

Contents

Tables and Figures

Preface and Acknowledgments

Advances in the technology of transportation and communications since midcentury have compressed the earth and bound once-distant nations into close association. Nations are increasingly dependent on one another for raw materials, manufactured goods, and services, and world economic progress depends, to an ever-increasing degree, on the mutual benefits stemming from international trade, travel, and investment.

Many factors contribute to economic and social progress, but mobility is especially important because the ingredients of a satisfying life, from food and health to education and employment, are generally available only if there is adequate means of moving people, goods, and ideas.

Transportation in developed countries has made possible the commercialization of agriculture, the specialization of industry, ready access to material resources, and a host of educational and cultural opportunities. In large areas of the developing countries, however, transportation is often poor or nonexistent. The lack of all-weather access is a prime factor in rural poverty, while poor transport is subjecting the world's great cities to paralyzing congestion and adding to the frustration of urban living.

The state of transportation in many parts of the world is deteriorating as sluggish economic conditions contribute to the neglect of maintenance and lessen the amount of investment funds available. Yet rising population, industrialization, urbanization, and the need for food, energy, and raw materials continue to call for greater transport capacity. There will be an additional 1 billion people on the planet by the end of the century, and financing the necessary transport system within the resource limits imposed by competing demands poses difficult problems.

This book examines the condition of world transport and its role in global food supply, the conduct of industry and trade, the operation of cities, and the opportunities and choices made available by the speed and economy of travel. The pervasive role of transportation makes high productivity in this area essential to the attainment of objectives in other sectors and will require revisions in both national and international policies to help complete an effective global network.

A major concern is the ability to meet the food requirements of a world in which millions of poor families live on the verge of starvation. The key is higher rural incomes, which require more land in production and more intensive cultivation of existing farmland. Both depend on adequate transportation. American agriculture demonstrates the importance of delivering fertilizer and other inputs on time and of getting crops to market. In developing countries, however, farmers are often unable to obtain supplies or to market what they produce. Great volumes of food move internationally to bridge the gap between areas of surplus and deficit, but even famine relief bogs down on local distribution networks. A world in which all people are adequately fed requires much higher levels of transport performance in vast areas of the developing world.

Industrial development imposes complex tasks on transportation systems. Enormous quantities of building materials, energy resources, ores, and metals move over the networks of the industrial nations, and transportation has become an integral part of the processes of production. The magnitude of the transportation investments made over a lengthy period by mobile countries indicates the task that other nations face as they seek a larger share in manufacturing and trade.

The economic well-being of nations also depends on the health, vigor, and education of its people, which in turn depend on transportation to provide access to jobs, services, schools, and business opportunities. The contribution of personal travel to development has generally been underestimated as the emphasis in transportation has continued to highlight the movement of freight. Cross-country comparisons of per capita GNP and annual travel volumes show, however, that high income levels are more closely related to passenger mobility than to goods movement. The finding has important implication for the future of the automobile and for the uses of telecommunictions as an extension of the transport system.

Movement is a special problem of giant metropolitan areas, where transportation is essential yet a major cause of congestion, air pollution, noise, and blight. The problems differ very little among the world's great cities, whose commuters share the same daily frustrations. Yet costly attempts to solve problems of urban transport by adding to capacity often fail because other aspects are overlooked, including the design and arrangement of cities, the importance of intermodal transportation systems, equitable financing, sound pricing policies, and the need for more dispersed patterns or urban living.

Projections of world growth, viewed in the light of already overburdened transport facilities, indicate the urgency of new strategies to keep pace with mounting demand. Solutions must be found on two different fronts, the first being transport technology, management, and the research and development efforts needed to arrive at improved supply-side solutions. The second is the demand side of the problem and the need to influence the volume and characteristics of the transport services required. Possible solutions on this side of the ledger include materials processing to reduce the handling of waste products; energy choices that are transport-conserving; biotechnology that reduces the need for fertilizer; urban design that avoids unmanageable concentrations of traffic; and the uses of telecommunications as an extension of the transport system.

Along with technological breakthroughs, there is the need for innovative financing. Transportation systems throughout the world are amassing deficits that make it difficult to maintain existing facilities or to replace obsolete plants and equipment. The prospects for relief lie in greater support from users, while Third World countries also need more international technical and financial assistance, both public and private. A world-wide user charge on some aspect of international trade may be one answer to providing a predictable and continuing source of help. The rationale for external aid lies in the fact that better transport that accelerates Third World development will create new markets for industrial countries and enable developing countries to achieve higher levels of living and to contribute more to world production and trade.

Transportation in space makes it possible to view the problems of earth transportation in perspective. Viewing the planet from an orbiting satellite reveals the anomoly of a world divided between the mobile and immobile nations. On one side of the globe are most of the people, and on the opposite side is most of the transportation. Much of humanity subsists in isolation, disconnected from the material resources and information essential to economic progress. The effect of immobility in the Third World is not only to perpetuate poverty but also to limit the economic potentials of the rest of the globe, which has become extremely sensitive to the state of the world economy. An international effort is needed to help make the earth more accessible and to engage the rich countries and the poor in a mutually beneficial joint venture to overcome the transportation gap.

This is one of a series of books that I have written over the past two decades while a senior fellow at the Brookings Institution and director of its Transport Research Program. The series has included *Strategy for Mobility, Distance and Development,* and *The Accessible City.* This work draws on the results of transport assignments on five continents, including missions for the World Bank, the Asian Development Bank, the United Nations, the Organization of American States, and the U.S. Agency for International Development. The study was first suggested by the Executive Committee of the Transportation Research Board, National Research Council, and special thanks are expressed to William N. Carey, formerly Executive Director of the Board, and to his successor, Thomas B. Deen. The book was written while I was a guest scholar at the Brookings Institution. Major typing and related tasks were performed by Jewelene Gaskins, Margaret Su, Cochita Acupanda, Gertrude Entenmann, and Theda Henle. The manuscript was edited by Jane Warth. I wish to thank them and the many others who helped make this book possible.

Transportation and World Development

One / A Global Overview

The twentieth century, which began with the horse and carriage, has extended transportation into space. The contrast symbolizes the degree to which mobility is revolutionizing the conduct of human affairs. Advances in the technology of moving people and goods (and in the delivery of information) underlie much of the world's economic and social progress. The new mobility has blurred national boundaries, expanded opportunities, altered life styles, and helped much of humanity to achieve previously unimagined levels of production and income. It also has affected international comparative advantage and has created structural changes in the world economy, which have helped support development in low-income countries and compelled difficult readjustments in many industrial nations. Just as transport promoted the unification of the United States and created regional and national networks of industry and agriculture, the same process is now taking place on a planetary scale.

Trends in World Transport

Gross world product increased about four-fold between 1950 and 1985, and this was accompanied by a sevenfold increase in international seaborne shipping and a sixtyfold increase in air travel. On land, the amount of rail freight grew to three and a half times the 1950 level, and the number of motor vehicles increased by a factor of six.[1] The rapid growth of international trade and travel has been the most dramatic aspect of the changing transport scene, resulting in a sudden increase in the interdependence of nations. Two out of every five acres of land under cultivation in the United States are growing crops for export. One out of every six workers in American industry is filling overseas orders. Four hundred major U.S. corporations doing business abroad realize more than a third of their sales overseas, and many do more than half their business with foreign customers.[2] Telephone calls between the United States and other countries reflect the dimensions of America's global involvement: in twenty-five years the number of U.S. overseas calls has increased from less than one million to more than two hundred million per year.

New patterns of comparative advantage and of global economic development have caused changes that are increasingly evident as auto-

Table One / World Growth and Transportation

	1950	1983–85
Population (billions)	2.5	5.0
Gross world product (trillions of 1980 dollars)	2.5	10.2
Merchants fleets (millions of gross tons)	93.0	425.0
International seaborne shipping (millions of tons loaded)	550.0	3,415.0
Rail freight (billions of ton-miles)	1.2	4.3
Motor vehicles (millions)	70.0	473.0
Air travel (billions of passenger-miles)	9.0	651.5
Telephones (millions)	90.0	508.0

Sources: United Nations, *U.N. Statistical Yearbook, 1983–84* (New York, 1986); Motor Vehicle Manufacturers Association, *Facts and Figures '85* (Detroit, 1985); Bureau of the Census, *Statistical Abstract of the United States*, 106th ed. (Washington, D.C., 1986), and World Bank, *World Development Report, 1986.*

mobiles, textiles, steel, electronics, and other industries move to new locations in the developing world. American, European, and Japanese joint ventures cover every conceivable line of activity from clothing and computers to automobiles, petrochemicals, frozen foods, hotels, grocery stores, banking, and fast-food chains. General Motors has joined with Toyota in California, and it also owns part of Suzuki and Isuzu Motors; Ford has teamed up with Toyo Kogyo; and Hondas are made in Ohio.

Europe's Airbus, assembled in Toulouse, has British wings, American engines, and a French cockpit. Boeing's new commercial jets have their origins not only in Seattle but also in Japan and Europe. Pan American Airways flies planes produced by six nations. Many U.S. farms and office buildings have Middle East owners, and even the egg is hatching global business as Japan and the United States cooperate with France and Brazil to supply Egyptian-based Saudi Arabian poultry producers. American hotel chains are proliferating worldwide, golden arches grace the streetscapes of the world's cities, and America depends increasingly on steel, shoes, and wine from its multiple trading partners. Far-flung international networks are now engaged in the production of cement, chemicals, fertilizers, medicines, and textiles, and joint ventures have internationalized silicon chips, subways, bread, and robots.

Economic uncertainties and the value of the dollar are affecting the economic fortunes of all nations, but world trade continues to expand, and business with developing countries becomes increasingly important. Nearly half of total U.S. merchandise exports represents deliveries to less developed countries and industrial nonmarket economies. While the growth of exports to Europe, Japan, and other industrial areas increased fourfold from 1920 to 1981, the increase in developing country purchases was nearly sevenfold. U.S. imports from the developing world increased over the same period by a factor of eleven. The importance of trade between the developed and the developing countries has led to extensive bartering arrangements to deal with the foreign exchange shortages of many trading partners. Aircraft parts are paid for in canned hams and leather coats, while countertrade arrangements for the sale of machinery accept payment in vodka and blue jeans.

In a typical year, the United States sells two-thirds of its wheat, half its fats and oils, and a fourth of its corn to foreign customers. Other developed countries, notably Canada and Australia, produce grain surpluses, bringing total world exports to over one hundred million tons, which is 50 percent greater than exports in the late sixties. The deficits in other parts of the world continue to increase, however, with Western Europe and Japan together requiring some forty million tons of food grain imports per year, and developing countries requiring another thirty million tons. China and the Soviet Union are adding millions more to the amount of imported wheat.

Global travel, too, has multiplied international passenger traffic and altered economic, political, and cultural contacts among nations. World meetings, student exchanges, international organizations, multinational business ventures, and shuttle diplomacy are the order of the day. The pervasive effects of foreign travel on attitudes and understanding can be judged by the fact that some 200 million passengers fly to international destinations every year. According to the U.S. Department of State, over the past four decades overseas business trips by Americans have increased eightfold, government missions have increased sixfold, and travel for educational purposes has more than doubled.

The Stages of Mobility

The advent of the global economy has taken us by surprise, and history helps to explain why. Throughout the ages humanity has become accustomed to living locally in a relatively static state. The invention of the wheel (in about 5,000 B.C. in what is now Iraq) marked the beginning of a breakthrough, but its effect on the radius of economic activity was extremely limited. Having discovered the advantages of rolling friction over sliding friction, people were content for centuries to push and pull wheeled vehicles, aided only by building roads and by harnessing animals that proved agreeable to the arrangement.

The first stage in the evolution of transportation, the age of immobility and poverty, went unchallenged for millennia and still dominates the lives of at least 2 billion people. The pattern of living under these conditions consists of primitive agriculture and handicraft industries, with a minimum of travel and access to information. The efforts of developing nations to break out of this initial stage of mobility continue to be thwarted by the same obstacles that plagued all generations before them. The transport symbols of traditional societies are dirt tracks, bullock carts, camels, crude country boats, and human beings toiling as beasts of burden.

The United States itself was subject to these same conditions not so many years ago. In the nineteenth century, commodities could not be moved overland more than twenty miles from their origin before the cost of transport became prohibitive. It was cheaper to move a ton of goods across the ocean to Europe than to move a ton ten miles through Pennsylvania. An oxcart might take three days to move thirty-five miles. In New England the farmers' shoes and clothing were made from home-fabricated materials, and almost everything consumed was the product of the locality. There could be no specialization without the ability to trade.

Finally came stage two, the period of transport mechanization and industrial development. In the early 1820s the partnership between people and animals began to give way to the application of steam power to the wheel. The first railroads made it possible for people to advance through the English countryside at the unheard-of speed of twenty miles per hour. In only a few decades it would be possible to move a ton of freight a mile on a teaspoonful of diesel oil. This second stage in the evolution of transportation has made its influence felt for some 150 years. It has been marked by large investments in overland road and rail facilities and in the development of canals and waterways. The greater radius of trade and travel made possible by the lower costs of transport enabled American entrepreneurs to trade New England shoes and textiles for cotton from the South and grain from the Midwest. The process of building an integrated nation had begun.

Stage three, which started with the emergence of the motor age in the twentieth century, accelerated progress toward higher levels of mobility, expanded the radius of human activity, and created nationwide systems of production and marketing. The motor age was initially confined largely to the United States, where it rescued farmers from rural isolation and enabled them to specialize and to adopt the latest scientific methods of cultivation. The motor vehicle expanded the suburbs, created new industries, opened up new sources of raw materials, and expanded markets. The Interstate Highway System facilitated nationwide travel, tourism, trucking, and the integration of many manufac-

Figure One / Untouched by the transport revolution. World Bank photo by Ray Witlin.

turing and service activities. Europe, Japan, and several other parts of the world followed the earlier U.S. lead into the motor age.

A fourth stage in the evolution of transportation and development began some forty years after the advent of the motor car. The air age is dominated by the passenger and cargo jetliners that link the world's major cities, and it is reinforced by the enormous capacity and low cost of intercontinental ocean transport by supertankers, container ships, and bulk cargo vessels. These operations by air and sea have been made increasingly practical as telecommunications have helped to facilitate the conduct of international business. Stage four is furthering the internationalization of economic activity and resulting in so extensive an interdependence among nations that the fortunes of the rich nations and the poor have become inextricably bound. The situation is the result of a sudden coincidence of technology and geography. A planet made up mostly of water and surrounded by air and space has been endowed from the outset with built-in rights-of-way for intercontinental transport. But only recently has the technology that could put these facilities to effective use been available. Aircraft and telecommunications rely on the atmosphere for cost-free passage, while ocean-going giants operate without charge on the world's shipping lanes. The effect has been to build bridges among nations and to promote a wider dispersal of economic activity throughout the world.

Figure Two / A containership in Pusan, Republic of Korea: the benefits of a planet that is three-fourths water. World Bank photo by Keum Yong Choi.

The earth is now on the threshold of stage five in the relation between mobility and development—the space age and the global economy. When the American space shuttle recently carried into orbit a satellite ordered by India to help supply telephone and other communication services for the subcontinent, this delivery over the Indian Ocean marked a logical progression in the evolution of transportation. By extending mobility beyond the earth, humanity has followed an orderly progression in the scope of its activities—once local, regional, and national—to international and global dimensions. A web of transport and communications has increased the possibilities of achieving a more prosperous and united world community.

But progress in space has illuminated the gaps in earth transport. Photographs taken by *Apollo 13* astronauts one hundred thousand miles from home dramatize the anomaly of an infinitesimally small planet that lacks a global transport system. Color composites from Landsat imagery at closer range reveal a world with two faces—one etched with roads, rails, and other channels of transport, and the other relatively unmarked by methods of movement. The new perspective shows the economic reality: a planet partly mobile and affluent and partly immobile and impoverished.

Figure Three / Air cargo: using nature's built-in rights-of-way. Japan Air Lines photo.

The urgency of the situation and the need for remedial action are brought home by one day's operation of a resource-sensing satellite. Such satellites circle the earth fourteen times every twenty-four hours. When the day's last trip is completed, there are 200,000 more people to feed and supply than when the day's first orbit began. These growth rates, combined with the material wants of the existing population, provide an indication of the enormous traffic loads that will have to be carried in the future.

The Unbalanced System

The transport revolution has affected most areas of the globe to some degree, but the principal changes in the speed and capacity of movement are heavily concentrated. The United States, Japan, and Europe own 80 percent of the world's motor vehicles, the Soviet Union accounts for half the world's railway freight, and the United States and the Soviet Union combined account for 77 percent of goods movement by rail. Half of the world's airline passengers are riding on U.S. domestic flights, and over 80 percent of all air travel is accounted for by North America, Europe, and the Soviet Union.

Many less developed areas have been largely untouched by the transport revolution. Their agriculture suffers from the lack of all-weather transport needed for access to markets and supplies. Industrial development is constrained by excessive transport costs and unreliable service

Table Two / World Area, Population, and Transportation

	Percentage of World Area	Percentage of World Population	Percentage of Motor Vehicles	Percentage of Ton-miles
Asia	20.3	58.3	14.1	13.5
Africa	22.4	10.9	2.3	2.0
North America	15.9	5.5	38.7	23.3
Latin America	15.1	8.3	7.0	1.3
Europe	3.6	10.6	31.6	8.5
Oceana	6.3	0.5	2.3	0.5
U.S.S.R.	16.4	5.9	4.0	50.9

Sources: Area: Bureau of the Census, Statistical Abstract of the United States, 1986 (Washington, D.C., 1985), p. 835; population: United Nations, U.N. Statistical Yearbook, 1982–83 (New York, 1982), p. xxx; motor vehicles: Motor Vehicles Manufacturers Association, Facts and Figures '86 (Detroit, 1985), pp. 34–35; rail freight: U.N. Statistical Yearbook, 1983–84 (New York, 1986), p. 55.

and by the lack of capacity to serve the needs of rapidly rising population. Land and other resources remain inaccessible, production and incomes lag, and rural education has been made impractical by poor transportations. Africa, Asia, and Latin America have 77 percent of the world's people and 58 percent of the area but only 17 percent of the rail freight, 5 percent of the motor vehicles (excluding Japan), and less than 10 percent of the paved highways. While most developed countries have at least one motor vehicle for every 10 persons, and many have one vehicle for 2 to 6 persons, poor countries have only one vehicle for 200 to 500 persons. A dozen countries containing half the population of the world own fewer than 2 percent of the world's motor vehicles. In China there is one motor vehicle for every 1,022 people.[3]

In much of the developing world, railroads are antiquated and obsolete, and roads are impassible in the monsoon. Construction work requires the laborious headloading of dirt and stone to the site. Men and women are pulling and pushing heavy carts, moving bulk materials on and off ships, and poling crude country boats laden with cargo. Nearly everyone engages in the movement of freight—by bicycle, bullock cart, camel and donkey, or simply by the strength of their own backs. Millions of trips are taken daily to transport water for the household from standpipes in city slums or from the village well.

The size of the mobility gap between the rich countries and the poor ones, and the relation between mobility and economic progress, can be seen in the comparison between gross national product per capita and transport facilities and traffic. A mobility index that combines available

Figure Four / Transporting water—a universal problem. World Bank photo by Ray Witlin.

data on transport facilities and the movement of passengers and freight has been constructed. Using an index number of one hundred to indicate levels of GNP and of freight and passenger mobility in France, it was found that nations with a per capita GNP (in 1979 dollars) of less than ten ($1,000) generally had a mobility index for freight and passenger transport in the single digits. Immobility and poverty go hand in hand. High levels of mobility, for freight or passenger travel, or both, are generally found only in those countries with per capita GNP above thirty ($3,500).

The mobility indexes help to quantify the differences among countries in the capabilities of their transport systems. It should be noted, however, that data describing the world's transportation facilities and operations lack consistency and vary considerably in reliability. In addition, it did not appear feasible to include domestic water transportation, which is especially important in several countries of Western Europe and Southeast Asia. Data on international transport were not included, except for air passenger services. Nevertheless, the broad dimensions of the transportation gap are clearly evident.

Comparing the situation in the United States with conditions in India

Table Three / Index of per Capita GNP and Mobility (France = 100)

Selected Countries	GNP per Capita	Travel Mobility	Freight Mobility
Switzerland	139	104	81
Sweden	119	96	151
Federal Republic of Germany	117	101	57
Belgium	109	88	117
Norway	106	55	107
United States	106	160	260
Netherlands	101	83	42
France	100	100	100
Canada	95	114	374
Australia	91	107	335
Japan	87	96	94
United Kingdom	63	78	47
Czechoslovakia	53	54	132
Italy	53	86	49
Spain	43	54	44
U.S.S.R.	40	34	229
Hungary	38	34	68
Venezuela	31	24	36
Yugoslavia	24	32	55
Argentina	24	32	114
Iran	32	10	10
Brazil	18	18	23
Mexico	15	14	42
Republic of Korea	15	8	16
Malaysia	14	11	26
Turkey	14	5	26
Ecuador	11	5	21
Colombia	11	6	47
Nigeria	6	5	5
Philippines	6	2	18
Egypt	5	5	13
Indonesia	3	3	5
Pakistan	2	3	10
China	2	3	16
India	2	5	26
Ethiopia	1	2	3
Bangladesh	1	2	3

Note: Data on a per capita basis include estimated passenger-miles per year by automobile, rail, and domestic air travel; miles of railway, ton-miles of railway freight, miles of roads, and numbers of trucks.

Sources: GNP per capita in 1979 dollars: World Bank, *World Development Report, 1981* (Washington, D.C., 1981), pp. 134–35. Air travel: United Nations, *U.N. Statistical Yearbook, 1981* (New York, 1981), pp. 598–607. Rail passenger and freight: Bureau of the Census, *Statistical Abstract of the United States, 1982–83* (Washington, D.C., 1982), pp. 880–81. Roads and trucks: International Road Federation, *World Road Statistics* (Washington, D.C., 1980). Water transport: not available.

illustrates the size of the transport discrepancy. If everyone in the United States decided to travel by automobile at one time, there would be 534 cars available for every 1,000 persons, and no one would need to ride in the back seat. Every 740 Indians would have to share one car. There are more trucks in Kentucky (population 3.6 million) than in all of India (population 750 million.) Communications are no better. If everyone in the United States wanted to watch television at once, two people could share each available set. If everybody simultaneously decided to telephone, only one person would have to wait. The situation in India would be quite different. Five hundred Indians would have to share a television set, and 2,500 would have to wait in line for the phone.

Road conditions also differ widely among countries. Switzerland, the Federal Republic of West Germany, Great Britain, and France have between two and three miles of road per square mile, and 90 to 100 percent of the mileage is paved. Many African countries, including Ghana, Niger, and the Ivory Coast, have only one tenth to one fifteenth as much mileage in relation to area, and the percentage of roads paved ranges from 3 to 17 percent.

The gap between the rich nations and the poor is widening, as indicated by comparing the foregoing passenger and freight indexes with those calculated for 1961 in my book *Strategy for Mobility*. Over the twenty-year period the poorest countries appear to have become relatively worse off compared to the middle- and high-income nations. Although there have been gains in the volume of freight moved by countries at the bottom of the income ladder, there has been a notable lack of any appreciable gains in passenger mobility over the span of two decades. Most countries have put more emphasis on the movement of goods and materials in their economic development programs, and often the ability of people to travel and communicate has been thwarted by the absence of travel facilities and the lack of telephone and other means of communication. Some of the reasons and remedies are discussed in later chapters, which conclude that economic and social progress may depend as much on moving people as on delivering freight.

Comparisons of income and mobility are not meant to imply that transportation by itself is capable of achieving economic development. It is a necessary but not sufficient element in the development process, and many costly transport undertakings have turned out to be extremely wasteful of resources because they were not accompanied by other actions to further economic progress. Many miles of roads in poor countries prove more useful for drying beans and peppers than for moving traffic. And in the United States, the Bureau of Public Roads concluded in the fifties that some 160,000 miles of rural highways had served no useful purpose and should be abandoned.

In some cases where the preconditions for takeoff are already present, the building of transport facilities provides the spark that activates an otherwise dormant economic potential. In other cases investments in transportation lead to little or no development because the other ingredients of successful farming or manufacturing were not available and were not supplied. But generally there is a close relation between transportation and economic development because mobility and access are the only means by which the ends in other sectors can be accomplished.

Transport Needs and Resources

For more than half the world that is still underdeveloped, transportation facilities fall far short of current needs and are totally incapable of supporting anticipated population growth. Ninety percent of that growth will be in poor countries. The number of people on earth is expected to increase from 5 billion in 1987 to over 6 billion within the next two decades. Eventually, 10 billion people may have to be supported before a stationary level of population is reached. Even if there were a fully effective population-control policy in force, it would take seventy-five years to bring the developing world population to an equilibrium level, and this level would be twice as high as when effective control policies were first adopted.[4]

If the world's poor were to enjoy substantially higher levels of consumption by the year 2000, assuming moderate growth rates, major efforts would be required to upgrade transportation. It is estimated that the world economy produced $11 trillion of goods and services in 1984 and that gross world product in the year 2000 will rise to $20 trillion (in 1979 dollars). This near doubling of the output of goods and services will create enormous additional needs for transportation. In the United States, the growth of population and income, and the shifting location of industrial and residential development, will increase and alter transportation requirements while new technology and the need for greater efficiency will accelerate the need to replace obsolete and overage facilities. But the impact of growth and development will be especially heavy in low-income countries that suffer the greatest transportation shortages yet are least able to marshal the needed financial resources and technical skills.

Of the 6 billion people expected to be living on the planet early in the twenty-first century, 5 billion will be in developing countries. Because of the closer international links created by transport and communications, poverty and lack of production in these areas have obvious implications for the United States and other developed countries. Without adequate transportation to support increased agricultural production in developing nations, food deficiencies will multiply pressures on world supplies and raise prices for consumers everywhere. Mobility is also essential if industrialization is to raise income and expand exports to pay for imports. And without greater access and mobility in low-income nations, resources needed by a growing planet will remain out of reach.

It is equally clear that much of humanity is unable to share in the accumulation of knowledge and technical progress because of the isolation resulting from constraints on travel. Poor transport means lack of schooling or exposure to new ideas, and the inability to find work or to perform the travel involved in holding a job. Limitations on travel also inhibit the conduct of business and the performance of the many services needed to assure prosperous farming and productive industries.

Problems in Common

The condition of transportation in poor countries poses the greater threat to supplying the urgent needs of a growing planet. But the already industrialized nations, despite high levels of mobility, are also being challenged physically and financially by current transport conditions. The United States, having invested heavily over a long period to attain high levels of mobility, finds that much of the system is obsolete or overcrowded, and overdue for replacement and modernization. The costs of upgrading the system are astronomical, while the availability of funds has declined with growing resistance to taxes and runaway budget deficits. Airports and airways are heavily congested, automobile commuter routes are jammed, many miles of highways and thousands of bridges are in disrepair, and urban public transit, even after some $30 billion of federal aid, has been unable to respond to changes in the geography of the urban region. Rail transport has begun to take on new life after years of neglect, but the industry has far to go before the backlog of needs and the drag of obsolete facilities can be remedied.

Everywhere transport operating deficits have become a drain on public resources. Most of the world's transport systems are unable to pay their way through user charges. Funding lags behind rising transport costs, and the social costs of traffic congestion and air pollution continue to inflict a penalty on the general public.

Transportation and growth problems have been intensified by the dependence of nearly all methods of movement on petroleum and by the effects of world oil price fluctuations on the cost of mobility. The transport sector consumes 25 percent of the world's energy and 50 percent or more of the global output of petroleum. Road transport is the major user

Table Four / World Population and Projections (Millions)

	1983	2000	Expected Increase
Developing countries			
Low income	2,342	3,154	812
Middle income	1,166	1,690	524
High-income oil exporters	18	33	15
Total	3,526	4,877	1,351
Industrial Economies	1,115	1,211	96
World total	4,641	6,008	1,447

Source: World Development Report, 1985 (Washington, D.C.: World Bank, 1985), table 19, pp. 210–11.

in the transport sector, accounting in most countries for 70 to 80 percent of the commercial energy used for mobility. The fivefold increase in the cost of energy over a period of one decade resulted in serious international payments problems, excessive debt, the global restructuring of the automobile industry, and the necessity for air transport to absorb billions of dollars in extra fuel costs and in capital outlays for more energy-efficient aircraft.

For the non-oil-producing, less developed countries, most of them poor, there have been the more devastating costs of oil imports. These costs have been a major burden on countries such as Brazil, the Philippines, Thailand, Pakistan, and Ghana. Altogether there are over seventy-five countries that have to import 50 to 100 percent of their petroleum needs.[5] Later the petroleum-producing countries experienced the disruptive effects of price declines and the inability to service the loans that had been negotiated on the assumption of high-priced oil.

The conflict between cities and automobiles also continues to have global impacts. Cities have become increasingly unliveable as the noise, pollution, and congestion of traffic persist despite efforts to expand public transit and build more roadway and parking capacity. The mayors of the world's great cities, meeting several years ago to discuss their mutual problems, expressed an almost universal concern over the deterioration of urban living. They attributed much of this to the transport sector. The mayors of Tokyo, Moscow, New York, Paris, and London each spoke of the need for more satisfactory standards of travel yet agreed that the costs were already excessive and were diverting public funds from badly needed schools, recreation, health services, and housing.[6] A comparable exchange of views among mayors of cities in poor countries confirmed that the congestion, poor accessibility, and assorted physical and social problems of such cities as Lima, Bangkok, and Manila varied from those of New York, Chicago, or Tokyo only in their greater severity and the less likelihood that resources would ever be available to overcome them.[7]

The deterioration of roads and streets has also become a global phenomenon, and the mounting cost of construction has made it impossible to keep pace with the need for replacing worn-out bridges and pavements. In the United States, rising costs and reduced energy consumption (hence lower fuel tax collections) have created a financial squeeze that has reduced expenditures for maintenance and replacement below the levels necessary to keep heavily traveled facilities in acceptable condition. And in the Third World a survey of eighty-five countries released by the World Bank in 1987 revealed that the backlog of economically warranted main-road rehabilitation was some $41 billion. Failure to concentrate more resources on maintenance over the next five to ten years would add further to the mileage requiring costly rehabilitation. Much of the capital invested in road construction during the boom years of the previous two decades might be lost. These figures did not include needed bridge repairs or the cost of maintaining the vast networks of secondary and local access roads.

The list of problems affecting transport around the world is lengthening. The accident toll is costing 50,000 lives each year on the highways of the United States, 90,000 in Europe, and 100,000 in developing countries. Millions of cars are recalled each year because of mechanical defects. Train derailments number in the thousands every year, airway and airport congestion is worsening, and poorly managed and overcrowded ports in many parts of the world cause vessels to wait weeks to be loaded or unloaded at a cost of many thousands of dollars a day per ship. The universal picture is one of mounting transport demand, accumulating physical backlogs, and growing resource restraints.

There is no diminution of the tasks to be performed: moving everlarger volumes of food, supplying the energy and raw materials for industry, getting greater numbers of commuters to work, and coping with constantly rising congestion levels in cities, at ports and airports, and on major intercity routes. Even the most conservative projections of freight and passenger traffic indicate the need to accelerate efforts to advance the state of transport in both rich countries and poor.

The state of world transport can thus be viewed from two perspectives. One is the physical condition of the subsystems that compose the total system—the intercontinental, intercity, local rural and urban networks. The other is the functional performance of the networks—how

Table Five / Per Capita Income, Selected Countries

	1983 Population (millions)	GNP per Capita (1983 dollars)
All Low-income Countries (35)	2,335	260
Ethiopia	41	120
Bangladesh	96	130
Nepal	16	160
Zaire	30	170
Burma	35	180
Tanzania	21	240
India	733	260
China	1,019	300
Ghana	13	310
Sri Lanka	15	330
Kenya	19	340
Pakistan	90	390
Sudan	21	400
All Middle-income Countries (59)	1,652	1,310
Senegal	6	440
Bolivia	6	510
Indonesia	156	560
Honduras	4	670
Egypt	45	700
Philippines	52	760
Nigeria	94	770
Thailand	49	820
Nicaragua	3	880
Costa Rica	3	1,020
Guatemala	8	1,120

transport is serving agriculture, industry, trade, personal opportunity, urban living, and regional growth. Both approaches help reveal how mobility is serving the development process and what physical and financial needs are dictated by the changing world economy.

The significance of such an appraisal stems from the widening gaps in income between the richer nations and the poor, and the urgent need to discover how these gaps might be reduced. There are thirty-five countries with 2.3 billion inhabitants whose average annual income is $260 per capita. There are fifty-nine middle-income countries that account for 1.6 billion people and their income per capita averages $1,310 per year. In contrast, nineteen industrial countries with 0.7 billion people enjoy income levels that average over $11,000 per capita. The income spread between people in the poorest countries and those in the richest is

(*continued*)

Peru	18	1,285
Turkey	47	1,240
Colombia	28	1,530
Brazil	130	1,880
Korea	40	2,010
Argentina	30	2,070
Mexico	75	2,240
South Africa	32	2,440
Yugoslavia	23	2,570
Israel	4	5,370
Hong Kong	5	6,000
All Industrial Market Economies (19)	*729*	*11,060*
Spain	38	4,780
Ireland	4	5,000
Italy	57	6,400
New Zealand	3	7,730
United Kingdom	56	9,200
Austria	7	9,250
Netherlands	14	9,890
Japan	119	10,120
France	55	10,500
Federal Republic of Germany	61	11,430
Canada	25	12,310
Sweden	8	12,470
Norway	4	14,020
United States	234	14,110
Switzerland	7	16,290

Source: World Bank, *World Development Report, 1985* (Washington, D.C., 1985), pp. 174–75.

from $120 per capita per year to $16,290. Such inequalities can hardly provide the conditions necessary for global prosperity or for peaceful relations among countries.

Many factors of geography, history, climate, and resources underlie the fortunes and misfortunes of nations. This book examines one set of circumstances in the total picture—the relation between the mobility and prosperity of the industrial countries and the immobility and poverty of nations that are isolated and disconnected from the rest of the world. History makes it clear that transportation, as a means to other ends, can have a pervasive impact on economic and social development. Full-scale efforts to improve mobility, applying recent advances in technology and management, could thus be a key to overcoming the hunger and poverty that afflict more than half the people on earth.

Two / Mobility and World Food Supplies

The world depends for its food on a global transportation network that supplies the farmer with seed and fertilizer, gets the crops to market, and bridges the intercontinental gap between areas of food surplus and deficit. The network consists of three different subsystems: the intercontinental connections, the dense web of transport facilities serving the agricultural sectors of high-income countries, and, at the other end of the line, the quite inadequate facilities that retard the modernization of agriculture in the developing countries where the numbers of people to be fed constitute more than half the world's population.

In the mid-eighties, world grain production hit record highs and the output of developing countries had increased 3 percent annually for a decade and a half. But population gains were nearly equal to production gains, so that output per capita rose only 0.5 percent per year.[1] The gap in calories per person persisted, with North Americans accounting for 3,612 calories a day, whereas the average for people in developing countries was less than 2,400. Some African countries had fewer than 2,000 calories per capita per day, and developing countries in the Far East reported 2,151 calories per day.[2]

To these statistics should be added the fact that most of the exported food goes to nations that contain less than 20 percent of the world's people. They include much of Western Europe and Japan. Yet Asia alone accounts for 50 percent of the people to be fed, and, when Africa and Latin America are added, the number of persons subsisting near or below the hunger line is 77 percent of humanity. For them, expanding world trade has not been a major benefit.

The World Outlook

The overall picture indicates that much of the world's exported foods go to affluent countries with trade balances that can pay the bill, and that such countries will continue to be heavily reliant on the United States and other nations with agricultural surpluses. But the unmet requirements of the developing world are also very large, and they will be much greater in the future. Producing more at home will be obligatory except for those countries where it is economical to engage in other activities capable of earning the foreign exchange to pay for food imports.

The importance of the intercontinental transportation system to world food supplies stems from the wide dispersal of agricultural production over the earth's surface, reflecting differences in climate, soil, topography, and development. These conditions are being compensated by a network of ocean transportation that links producers in the United States, Canada, and other productive agricultural areas with the increasing numbers of people who live in food-deficit countries.

Problems in food supply are reflected in the uneven distribution of arable land in relation to population. For example, Japan has only about one-tenth of an acre of arable land per capita, whereas the United States has twenty-four times as much. East Asia has only one-eighth as much arable land per person as the United States.[3] There is also considerable food traffic in specialized items or products grown in relatively few areas of the world. Thus, while the United States was well-supplied with food, the Port of New York and New Jersey in 1980 handled nearly four million tons of food imports to balance out the U.S. diet. Incoming cargoes included thousands of tons of fish, fruits, vegetables, coffee, salt, and sugar.[4]

The vital role of the international food transportation network is illustrated by Europe's trade in fruits and vegetables. The European Economic Community (Belgium, Luxembourg, France, the Federal Republic of Germany, Italy, and the United Kingdom) is able to maintain an ample supply of lettuce, tomatoes, fresh vegetables, and fresh fruits throughout the year because efficient networks of sea and air transport now furnish supplies during the winter months. Major countries around the Mediterranean, with half their population in agriculture, depend for a livelihood on the production of oranges, grapes, and vegetables for export to the north. The community is now the largest importer of fresh fruits and vegetables in the noncommunist world, accounting for 55 percent of world fruit imports and 60 percent of world vegetable imports. Countries such as Egypt, Greece, Israel, Morocco, Spain, and Turkey share in this trade, which has increased at a rate of 4 percent a year in volume and 22 percent a year in value for a number of years.[5] Fruit and vegetable exports to Europe are also arriving from over one hundred other countries, including Australia, New Zealand, the United States, and nations in the Caribbean.

Projections to the year 2000 indicate the growing importance of international trade in grains. Import requirements of Western Europe and Japan are expected to rise to one hundred million tons a year. Other countries will probably be purchasing an additional seventy million tons. The major deficit areas are Western Europe, Japan, and the Soviet Union. They may consume about fifty million tons of grain above the amount they produce at home. The developing areas of the world may add another thirty million tons to the overall deficit.

In the mid-eighties the world's ten leading food exporters transported 102 million tons of wheat annually. The major suppliers were the United States and Canada, which accounted for over half the total tonnage of exported wheat moving over the intercontinental network. Other major suppliers included France, Australia, and Argentina. Their principal customers were the Soviet Union, China, and Japan. Large quantities of wheat also went to the developing world, including Brazil, Egypt, Morocco, Iran, and Korea.

The amount of corn that moved over the international food network totaled some sixty-four million tons for the ten leading exporters, two-thirds of the total from the United States. Other major suppliers included Argentina, Thailand, and France. Leading importers included the Soviet Union, Japan, Spain, Portugal, Belgium, and the Netherlands, as well as a number of less developed countries, including the Republic of Korea, Mexico, and China.

Exports from the United States and other countries producing surplus grain can be expected to continue playing an important role. But with 90 percent of future world population growth occurring in the less developed countries, it is questionable how much of their future deficits could be made up by transporting food from abroad. Even if external food production were of sufficient magnitude to meet the need, distribution would require extensive improvements in rural transport networks, and the amounts of foreign exchange involved would be far greater than most developing countries would be willing or able to pay. All signs point to the need for greater food output in developing countries if world requirements are to be met.

Recent famine in Africa suggests that hunger poses a greater threat today than it did a century ago. High rates of population growth combined with drought could mean critical food deficits in the years ahead. If the world is to produce and deliver enough food to meet an expected 90 percent increase in demand by the year 2000, output will have to expand at near-record rates. There is evidence that such accomplishments can be realized. The Green Revolution has brought spectacular results in many parts of the Third World that as recently as 1950 were barely keeping pace with increasing population. Since then, the growth rate for world food production has doubled. Further gains, however, will require an increase in the amount of land under cultivation, as well as significant increases in the productivity of land already being farmed. Reliable all-weather transport will be needed in both cases: to provide access to new lands and to make it possible to deliver seed, fertilizer, pesticides, and other inputs for intensive cultivation. In addition, as the

Global 2000 Report to the President concluded, if areas of surplus are to help supply areas suffering deficits, world trade in food may have to be 60 percent higher in the year 2000 than the record mid-seventies levels.

Increasing lengths of haul will add to the problem. At one time, most people obtained a large part of what they ate in the immediate vicinity of where they lived. Soon half the people in the world will be living in urban areas that rely on sources that are often distant from the city. Transportation will thus become increasingly important in meeting total food requirements.

The Relevance of American Experience

The United States enjoys an unusual combination of favorable conditions which enables it not only to produce most of its own food but also to function as the world's major food exporter. Mobility plays a key role. American farmers have ready access to tools, supplies, and well-organized markets, and they have made transport an integral part of the production process itself, using transport linkages to further specialization and productivity.

Food consumption in the United States involves the delivery of 1,286 pounds annually for every one of the nation's nearly one quarter of a billion people. An average dinner served in Boston may have been transported ten thousand miles, with meat from the Midwest, vegetables from California and Texas, flour from Minneapolis, sugar from Louisiana or the Philippines, and coffee from Colombia or Brazil. (In rural Thailand or Indonesia, an average dinner may have been transported fewer than one hundred miles.)

The great bulk of America's food is now delivered to the consumer by various types and sizes of trucks, many especially designed for their particular food-carrying purposes. One out of every five trucks in the United States is used in agriculture. Refrigerated trucks, livestock carriers, and tank trucks for milk, molasses, and vegetable oils supply the market.

The truck and modern highway are responsible not only for moving the food but also for revolutionizing the organization and methods of food production. Many farms specialize in doing one thing on a large scale—raising hogs, producing eggs, or growing oranges. One multi-farm network, for example, produces half a million eggs a day. The farms, spread over four states, raise chickens that are delivered regularly by truck to one hundred destinations. Deliveries have to be made within ten hours to avoid high mortality rates.[6]

The speed and reliability of road transport have had comparable effects on the production of meat. Cattle, once driven on hoof to the

Figure Five / Truck trailers with fruit from Florida ride a rail piggyback train. Association of American Railroads photo.

railroad and sent to Chicago stockyards, now travel by truck to local markets with minimum loss of weight. Stock raisers can choose the place and time for marketing. Semitrailers, which carry as many as 40 cattle or 160 hogs, are an integral part of the industry's organization and marketing operations.

Animals have become frequent travelers, and cattle, especially, are likely to make multiple trips during their lifetime. Calves produced in one area are transported elsewhere for fattening, and millions move into feed lots in the Corn Belt states or as far west as the Pacific region from distant eastern and southern locations. Shipments to and from these states generate a total movement of sixteen million head per year. About 95 percent of all livestock trips are by truck, which minimizes handling problems, protects animals from adverse weather, and reduces transit time. About one-third of total animal weight is lost in processing, so that meat-packing plants are located near sources of supply to avoid the cost of transporting waste.

Rail and water transportation moves most of the grain and grain products that are basic items in the food budget and that represent major farm transport tonnages. About three-quarters of the annual grain harvest is moved by rail, and one-fourth by water. Railroads handle as many as thirty-five thousand carloads of grains a week—over one hundred million bushels. Much of the crop is moved into storage areas, but large volumes are exported and moved directly by rail and barge to the ports. Grain for domestic use reappears on the rail system at a later date in the form of flour, soybean meal, cornstarch, and corn syrup.[7]

The food transport network also delivers approximately fifty million tons of commercial fertilizers each year in the United States, together with the raw materials for their manufacture, including natural gas, ammonia, sulphur, and phosphate rock. Also required are liming materials for application on acid soils. Great quantities of limestone must be transported to the mills and hauled to food-producing areas. Millions of tons of phosphate rock are also transported every year, and sulphur, a key fertilizer ingredient mined in Texas and Louisiana, is shipped to over one hundred plants in forty-two states to be made into sulfuric acid and transported to fertilizer plants.[8] About 90 percent of the phosphate rock used for fertilizer is mined in central Florida, but the superphosphate fertilizers processed from the rock are used primarily in the Corn Belt states that extend from Ohio and Indiana westward to Illinois, Iowa, and Minnesota. Some of the rock is shipped from Tampa across the Gulf to the Mississippi Delta, processed there, and transferred to barges that move up the Mississippi River. Some rock moves all the way from Florida to the farm states by rail. Transport costs are reduced by balancing the movement of fertilizer in 100-car-unit trains with return loads of grain. Because most plant nutrients are applied to the soil in a three-week period during the spring, storage capacity in the farm states plays an important part in reducing peak transport requirements.

The food processing industries play a major role in reducing food losses and in assuring year-round supplies of perishables. Four hundred plants scattered throughout the country in nearly all of the states are engaged in making 90 billion cans a year for various types of food. Another 310 billion bottles and other glass containers are made annually. Assuring year-round supplies of fruits, vegetables, and juices requires enormous amounts of paper and cardboard for packaging these and all the other groceries that arrive in boxes and bags to line supermarket shelves.

The transportation network serving American agriculture has been built at a heavy cost over a period of many years. But costs continue to rise with the growing difficulties of maintaining and adapting the system to changes in farm technology. The more than two million miles of local roads off the main federal-aid system were built in the early part of the century, when transportation was by horse-drawn vehicles. Roads are often narrow, winding, and ill-adapted to the trucks and farm

Figure Six / Loading grain on barges in Kansas City, Kansas. U.S. Department of Agriculture photo by Murray Lemmon.

equipment that move over them today. In addition, it has been estimated that more than half of all bridges on the local road network are deficient—a total of 170,000 bridges in all. As the size of farms has increased, so has the number of large tractor-trailers carrying produce to market, and consolidated farms use equipment that is much larger and heavier than in earlier years. These conditions have impeded the movement of agricultural traffic in many states. Much greater financial support will be required if rural transport systems are to be repaired and replaced to serve current farming practices.[9] Developing countries will need to avoid large-scale operations that involve excessive loads on roads and bridges, as well as farm specialization on the U.S. scale that requires excessive dependence on all-weather rural transport.

Mobility and Third World Agriculture

In the developing areas of the world, poor or nonexistent roads and dependence on animal transport and headloading have left vast areas engaged in primitive methods of cultivation entirely outside the market economy. In the past two decades there have been extraordinary efforts to modernize rural transport, but millions of farmers remain as isolated as their American counterparts of the nineteenth and early twentieth centuries. Lack of transportation remains a primary reason for low productivity, lack of trade, and meager incomes.

India and China demonstrate the critical importance of overcoming these conditions. They contain 40 percent of the world's people and may have a combined population of over 3 billion before a stationary level is reached. The extent to which these two countries are able to meet their own food requirements, and the degree to which they draw on global food supplies, are important factors affecting the world food outlook. At the present time the poor condition of rural transport in both countries warns that much greater efforts will be required to meet the changing needs of these increasingly populous areas.

India has made substantial improvements in transportation in the past two decades, and its agricultural output has been sharply upward. Food grain production rose from 55 million tons in 1950 to 150 million tons in 1985. It is estimated that half of the increase during the seventies was attributable to the use of fertilizer (delivered mainly by combining rail and bullock-cart transportation). There was a fifty-fold growth in the application of plant nutrients in twenty-five years. Yet only a third of the total area under cultivation was fertilized. The growth of India's population to one billion people by the year 2000, however, will require much greater output and far greater transportation of plant nutrients.

In earlier years, a higher rate of farm output could be achieved by extending the area under cultivation, but now the scarcity of land makes the possibilities of such extensions quite limited, and further increases in output will depend mainly on more intensive cultivation, which means the delivery of more fertilizer and other inputs.[10] However, delivery systems now in use are hardly equal to the task. The railroads are often called upon to deliver fertilizer over very short distances, a service they cannot perform well. The result is endless delays and a major obstacle to getting supplies to out-of-the-way places. Fertilizer shortages at the village level are consequently encountered through much of the country, and the use of fertilizer varies by a wide margin between areas well-served and poorly served by truck. The Punjab, with good roads, is well supplied, but in remote locations such as Assam, only 5 percent of the total cropland is fertilized.[11]

The reasons for the low productivity of agriculture in backward areas are said to be the absence of sufficient tube wells for irrigation, the short supply of fertilizer and other inputs, and the lack of credit facilities. But there is good evidence that lack of mobility is contributing to these conditions. It is extremely difficult to market produce or to obtain needed inputs where farms are far removed from an all-weather road or from any road at all. Isolated farmers cannot drill tube wells without the accessibility required to transport the drilling equipment to the site. Without transport at reasonable cost, it is not possible to obtain delivery or meet the cost of seed, pesticides, fuel, and other inputs that modern agriculture requires.

Access to market is not simply a matter of road conditions, however, but of distance to be traveled. For example, although two-thirds of the villages in the Indian state of Uttar Pradesh have a road connection, half these villages are five to ten miles from an important market, and one out of five is more than ten miles from a major center. Bullock carts, camels, and headloading make it difficult to move the volume of produce necessary to yield a reasonable return for the effort.

The attempt to benefit from increased milk production is an example of the frustrations encountered when roads are poor. Milk producers living on bad roads find it uneconomical to market their surplus and have to dispose of it locally for whatever they can get because the milk collector, who often travels by bicycle, cannot carry enough on a bad road to make the trip pay. He is able to carry at least twice as much on a good road and, therefore, avoids farms with poor access. But now a well-organized effort is being made to shorten the milk run and to make the most of India's limited rural transport. A nationwide plan has been put into effect for collecting milk by trucks that travel on main roads to pick up the cans that 2 million farmers carry to designated collection points every day. This national milk cooperative effort includes ten thousand villages that supply two and a half million quarts a day to Delhi, Bombay, and other consuming centers. The network is operated by the nation's primary milk producers, with technical and financial assistance from government and international organizations. Even the landless poor who own one or two cows can participate in this means of increasing milk supplies and augmenting rural incomes.[12]

Still, the magnitude of the road problem is a serious obstacle to feeding India. Most of the million miles of roads are unsurfaced, and much of the network consists of animal paths and cart tracks. Even on the national highway system of primary routes, a third of the mileage has only one lane. Altogether, 400,000 of India's 600,000 villages have no all-weather roads.[13] The Fifth Plan had expected that road links would be provided to 29,000 villages with 1,500 or more people, but fewer than half this number actually received the roads that were programed. In the eighties, it is planned that the remaining villages in this class will be connected to the main road system, and that half the villages with 1,000 to 1,500 people will also be supplied with a road link. Although the local road budget was quadrupled over the previous plan period, much greater outlays will be needed before the ratio of passable roads to cultivated areas can approach the levels targeted.[14]

Figure Seven / Delivering milk to a collection center in India. World Bank photo by Peter Muncie.

China to date has had notable success in feeding its 1 billion people through an effective combination of intensive cultivation using organic fertilizers, local transport (carts and human energy), and food distribution through a system of basic rations. A food ration is supplied to all consumers through the allocation of locally grown crops and the maintenance of a local food reserve. The surplus is sold to the national food ministry, which collects, processes, stores, and distributes some fifty million tons of grain per year, mainly by rail and water transport.[15]

Food supplies per capita have not increased for a number of years in China, but a growing number of people have enough to eat and the country manages to export rice.[16] (If India had a rationing program, according to one estimate, all Indians would be able to enjoy an adequate basic ration with only 6 percent more food than is now available.)[17] The volume of food that will have to be carried on China's transportation system in the future will increase with population growth, rising incomes, and the changing structure of the Chinese economy. The growth of industrial production will mean larger numbers of people living in cities more distant from sources of food, and urbanization is likely to increase the volume and variety of what is eaten. Industrialization may also require the railways to concentrate more on moving raw materials and other heavy freight, leaving a much larger part of agricultural marketing to trucks. But the mileage of good roads in China is limited at the present time, and the number and capacity of trucks will need to be substantially increased. Truck transport in China has been carrying less than 5 percent of the freight volume moved by rail.[18]

The situation in India and China, added to the serious outlook for Africa and many parts of Latin America, warns that rural transport requirements in developing countries will be far greater if the food transport network is to open up more land as well as permit more intensive cultivation. According to the Food and Agriculture Organization, the world is using only about 57 percent of the land potentially available for crops, but the areas still unused (46 percent in Latin America and 17 percent in sub-Saharan Africa) are especially deficient in roads, and road-building would present special problems because of adverse climate and topography.[19]

In the United States there are four miles of road for every square mile of arable land, and 80 percent of the mileage is surfaced. If this ratio were applied to the estimated 2.7 million square miles of arable land in use in developing countries in the mid-eighties, the required network would total some 10 million miles. The cost would be in the tens of billions of dollars. In addition, timely and continuous maintenance is essential, at a cost in 1980 that was about $2,500 to $5,000 a mile. Where maintenance is neglected, it may cost ten times as much to repair the damage. The loss is not only in the cost of the road but also in the high vehicle-operating costs incurred on roads in poor condition.[20]

Transportation for agriculture requires not only better roads but more trucks. The slow pace and limited capacity of animal-drawn carts often make it impossible to obtain on-time delivery of essential farm inputs, or leave the cultivator at the mercy of overworked railways during harvest periods. In European countries there is generally one truck for every 20 to 40 people. Canada and Japan have a truck for every 10 people. At the other extreme, Bangladesh has one truck per 4,000 inhabitants, and Afghanistan has one per 1,000. Both India and Indonesia have only one truck for 600 persons. If the developing world were to have half as many trucks in relation to people as France, they would need seventy million units, as compared to the twelve million now in use.

The use of trucks in the cooperative marketing plan for milk in India suggests that comparable arrangements might be made in the rural areas of developing countries to permit regular pickup of other farm output. Produce brought on foot or bicycle to subcenters could then be trucked to regulated markets, and the farmer paid for each day's supply of fruits and vegetables. The produce, sorted and crated, could then be brought to the main markets in the cities. An important aid to truck operation would be readily available loans to finance truck purchases over an extended period of time, for without such arrangements it is impossible for many would-be operators to pay the high initial cost of truck ownership.

Transportation and Rural Development

The fortunes of farming depend on a wide variety of conditions that are necessary to improve rural living conditions and income levels. Farm incomes are derived not simply from cultivating the fields but from the availability of schools, clinics, potable water, electric power, shops stocked with consumer goods, and jobs in local industry. All of these facilities and services are dependent on reliable transportation. Teachers often refuse to serve in villages if it is necessary to stay there overnight. They prefer villages with a road that permits them to commute by bicycle from a nearby town. Farmers are also in trouble. They cannot grow fruit and vegetables that would permit them to earn more money unless they can be assured of fast and reliable transport to market. Veterinarians and literacy workers shun the village that is not served by a good road, and it is even difficult to find a suitable bride because prospective in-laws refuse consent if it involves repeated visits over intolerable roads.

The variety of measures called for to increase the economic viability of the rural community is now recognized by international agencies, which combine projects in multipurpose efforts to improve the total rural environment. Programs for village access roads are tied to irrigation projects, school construction, power networks, and communications, all of which combine to create new activity and income, which is ultimately reflected in traffic that justifies the roads.

In Equador a rural development program undertaken with World Bank support included road-building, water supply, electrification, health services, and agricultural credits. In Nigeria feeder roads have been combined with agricultural extension services, fertilizer supplies, plant protection methods, and irrigation works. Rural road construction in Syria has been part of a package of tube-well construction and drainage facilities designed to halt the spread of salinity on adjacent farmlands.[21] An Inter-American Development Bank aid package for rural development in Colombia, involving a land settlement program covering one-fifth of the nation's cultivated area, included main highways, farm roads, bridges, schools, hospitals, antimalaria drugs, aerial photography, reforestation, and veterinary training.

The Republic of Korea has been conducting a nationwide program of rural development. The New Community Movement focuses on increasing rural incomes in thirty-four thousand villages through government-assisted projects for public infrastructure and services, home improvement, and the creation of small-scale industrial activities. With better transportation it is possible to engage in rice and barley production, which requires irrigation, fertilizers, and improved marketing arrangements. It has also become feasible to develop a fisheries industry. The Korean program has strengthened local management capabilities, and villages have contributed labor to match the value of government materials and financial assistance.[22]

One of the underlying problems of rural areas, the lack of communications with the outside world, can now be resolved with the help of modern telecommunications. A primary function of road transport in the countryside is the movement of information. In many remote locations it is possible to realize some of the advantages of transport by the use of communication satellites that provide telephone, television, and other information services years before all-weather transport can be made available. Technical assistance for farm operators, literacy programs, classroom instruction, health-care services, weather reports, and market information can all be delivered by the new networks.

The possibilities of overcoming the isolation of India's rural villages were demonstrated by the communication satellite experiment in rural education. The Satellite Instructional Television Experiment (SITE) was designed to furnish twenty-four hundred villages with community receiving sets for televised programs from a Delhi ground station, with direct telecasting to village sets. The physical task included finding twenty-four hundred villages with electricity and road access to permit the antenna and set to be installed. It was necessary to visit ten thousand villages before finding enough candidates with electric power and adequate road access. Because roads were hardly discernable, it was often difficult to find the same villages again to get the television receivers installed.

The program was carried on for a one-year period, with the help of maintenance crews that were allotted one hundred villages each to be serviced by jeeps carrying spare parts and replacement television sets. Transportation provided important support for communications, as crews were kept busy traveling to remote villages where rats had chewed cables, mice had feasted on speaker cones, and lizards periodically short-circuited the system.

Television in India had previously been limited to the immediate vicinity of Delhi and Bombay, but SITE made it possible to design programs specifically aimed at the needs of impoverished rural people. The experiment resulted in many changes in village life. School attendance increased, children found new interest in making things that had been demonstrated on television, and many more people began to visit extension agencies and other sources of information to further their understanding of subjects treated in the daily telecasts.

The potentials of overcoming rural isolation through telecommunications are measured by the fact that in developing countries there is often less than one telephone per 100 people, compared to sixty to seventy per 100 people in most developed countries. In 1981 the Pakistan telephone system had about a third of a million subscribers in a nation of 85 million people. The waiting list was as large as the total numbers being served, but this reflected only the backlog in areas that were already provided with telephone service. Business and household demand elsewhere was not even recorded. Even where telephones have been installed, available lines are so overworked that attempts to place a call must be repeated continually, adding to the congestion of the system.

A World Bank survey indicates that rural telephone service is generally limited to a pay phone or to a public phone installed in a village store, school, or post office, or in the home of a teacher, missionary, or chief. Although many urgent personal and business calls are completed in this way, there are serious drawbacks to using the service. Patrons must travel considerable distances to the phone, lines are often busy, the voice quality is poor, and conversations cannot be held in private. There is also a reluctance to go to the home of the teacher or chief, and people are deterred by lack of familiarity with the use of a phone. Also, a person receiving a call must be located and summoned to the phone, generally some distance away, which adds to the frustration.[23]

A Summary View

Global interconnections are making it possible to bridge the gap between the world's increasing number of food-deficit countries and a limited number of nations that are producing a surplus. Great quantities of grain, in particular, move over the life lines on which a growing number of food-deficit countries now depend. But as world population continues to increase and as giant cities demand additional sustenance, there are growing uncertainties about the long-term viability of present methods of supply. Many countries short of foreign exchange need to reduce their dependence on outside sources of food, and conditions favorable to local farming need to be exploited to help feed growing numbers of people and to help raise rural incomes. Food-exporting countries may also be vulnerable to soil erosion, drought, and other weather conditions that make it prudent for importing nations to supplement overseas sources with local harvests.

World food needs will increase rapidly in the coming years as population and incomes rise and as efforts are made to overcome the dietary deficiencies of existing poorly nourished populations. The move to the cities will continue to lengthen supply lines and to require greater volumes of produce to be hauled from rural to urban areas. Many elements will have to be included in a successful strategy to assure that the world has enough to eat, ranging from adequate price incentives and farm loans to irrigation, power, soil nutrients, and technical assistance. The responsibility of the transportation sector is to make possible the other elements that contribute to improving agriculture and rural development, hence to raising rural incomes. The improvement of rural roads and the expansion of trucking services are high on the list of global transport priorities if food deficiencies are to be overcome.

There are signs that the poor countries will be able to avoid some of the lengthy and costly programs that were needed in the United States and other developed countries to achieve the twentieth-century revolution in agriculture. Among the helpful aids are new sources of renewable energy, rural telecommunications, and the possibility, through biotechnology, of growing crops under adverse soil and moisture conditions, and without the aid of commercial fertilizer. These and similar innovations suggest that solving transportation problems is no longer simply a matter of supplying more capacity, but of changing the nature of the demand. Storage and processing are substitutes for moving produce to market at the harvest, and solar power may eliminate the need to transport wood and kerosene. These solutions on the demand side, combined with innovations in food production methods, may help to meet the transportation requirements of Third World agriculture.

In summary, mobility and accessibility are critical to agriculture, but also to the rural development on which agricultural progress depends. The importance of extending all-weather transport and supplemental communications is increasing rapidly with the growth of the rural population and with the greater numbers of people living in the cities. It is also apparent that while some countries can be said to be virtually self-sufficient in food, this means self-sufficiency in the economic sense of supply being in balance with demand—the amount that consumers can afford. In a nutritional sense, there is extreme imbalance, and millions of the world's people remain undernourished. The future food requirements of the planet would be magnified if the global objective were to assure that all people had enough to eat.

Finally, rural mobility and accessibility are essential to forging the necessary links with the urban-industrial sector, an exchange that is vital to both. For it is the countryside that feeds the cities, and urban industry that supplies the inputs for scientific agriculture. The next chapter will review the ways in which mobility is relied upon to feed the factories of the industrial world, and how the expansion of industrial traffic in Third World countries will be dictating future transportation system requirements.

Three / Supporting Industrial Development

The transportation systems that support the industrial and manufacturing activities of the United States and other high-income countries have been built over a long period of time at a very heavy cost. Now the growth of industry in the world's developing areas, which is essential to increasing income levels, is running into serious transportation bottlenecks. The global spread of industrial activity is well underway as some sixty-five newly industrializing nations are adding their output to the twenty-five nations already industrialized. But to date the new manufacturing activity, concentrated in the major cities, depends mostly on sales in the cities themselves and on the intercontinental transport network. Ocean shipping allows low-cost delivery of materials and air transport makes it possible to reach export markets quickly.

In the long run, however, neither the immediate urban surroundings nor the existing export markets will be sufficient to support an expanding manufacturing sector. There will be a need for wider domestic markets as well as for trade with other developing nations, where half the world's consumers live. Activating those markets involves intercity and rural transport systems that can support domestic development and provide links between the cities and their hinterlands. The complex freight systems serving the affluent nations provide evidence of how much transportation it has taken to meet the needs of modern industry, and they suggest the nature of the tasks that confront Third World countries as they further their manufacturing activities.

The Overall Picture

The newly industrializing countries face an inevitably heavy freight burden, and its magnitude and nature can be roughly approximated on the basis of what has occurred in countries that have experienced the process. That experience will also show how some of the burden can be avoided or, if not avoided, at least handled more expeditiously and at lower cost. The principal tasks will involve not only the movement of heavy bulk materials but also the integration of freight carriage with the actual operations of manufacturing plants and the successful marketing of goods and services.

An industrial transport network makes it possible for numerous factories producing parts and components to be linked with the assembly plants that turn out finished products. In the process, materials repeatedly travel over the transport system as they move from their original state through intermediate stages to their final form. This multiple trip-taking, which is typical of everything from chemicals to computers, explains why an industrial nation such as the United States moves thirty tons of freight per capita every year and runs up a freight bill of $750 million a day.

Every country moves a certain number of ton-miles of freight per dollar of goods and services produced. In a geographically large economy such as the United States, about two and a half ton-miles of freight service is required for every dollar of gross domestic product (in constant 1967–69 dollars). Ratios of transportation and output computed for other nations on the same constant-dollar basis reveal substantial differences among countries. The Soviet Union, with its great land area and heavy volumes of primary products such as coal and ore, generates nearly five ton-miles of freight traffic per dollar of output. The small countries of Western Europe, by contrast, generate one ton-mile or less per dollar of output. Japan has a comparable transport to product ratio. Although there are differences among countries, each maintains a fairly stable ratio over time.

Domestic figures tell only part of the story. International transportation is an additional factor that raises total requirements for many countries. An estimated sixteen trillion ton-miles of ocean shipping is now being generated annually worldwide. Supertankers, giant bulk cargo carriers, and container ships have multiplied the flow of materials and manufactured goods among nations in recent years, adding to the total amount of freight movement required to sustain an industrial economy, but providing a cost advantage for countries well-served by ocean transport. Nations that require only one ton-mile of domestic freight transport per dollar of output may generate another two ton-miles in international trade.

The network of freight transportation services supporting the United States and other industrial economies illustrates the magnitude of goods movement needed to sustain complex industrial societies. A relatively small number of bulk commodities dominates the demands of industry. In the United States, 75 percent of the rail tonnage is generated by shipments of coal, lumber, agricultural products, paper, chemicals, stone, glass, and miscellaneous minerals. Inland waterways also carry large quantities of bulk material, and coal and oil account for 60 percent of the tonnage moved. Much the same pattern is found elsewhere. In the Soviet Union, two-thirds of the tonnage is industrial materials, including coal and coke, building materials, petroleum, and ores. At the other end of the production process, a high-consumption society moves a great variety of finished items to wholesale and retail outlets. They include electrical equipment, textiles, clothing, household goods, and other manufactured items.

The distribution of freight among modes varies with geography and public policy as well as with economic development. Large land masses tend to rely on railroads, and this is more pronounced where official policy restricts the use of trucks. Railroads carry about 60 percent of the freight traffic in the Soviet Union, 46 percent in Pakistan, 45 percent in the Republic of Korea, and 67 percent in India.[1] In countries that can use water transport effectively, railroads are less important. Japan generates 50 percent of its freight ton-miles by ship and barge, and 13 percent by rail. It can be said as a general rule that with increasing stages of economic development, the percentage of freight traffic moving by rail declines, while the total amount of rail traffic increases. Road transport always increases substantially as a percentage of the total as well as in absolute amounts. For example, forty years ago U.S. railroads carried two-thirds of all intercity freight traffic. Recently this figure has been closer to one-third, but the total ton-miles transported by rail has risen sharply. Truck transport's share of the total during the same period increased from 10 to 24 percent, while total truck ton-miles increased more than tenfold.

Lessons from the United States

The task of keeping America's complex economy functioning involves the movement of an estimated 7.4 billion tons of freight per year, including both intercity and local movement. (Trucks move 2 billion tons, water transport another 2 billion, pipelines 1.9 billion, and railroads 1.5 billion.) The trend in the total has been steadily upward. Freight transport in the United States is five times the volume (in ton-miles) that moved forty years ago. This increase in goods and material hauling was in response to a quadrupling of GNP in constant dollars. The output of American railways has nearly tripled; truck traffic is eleven times the 1939 volume; and inland water traffic is more than four times greater.[2] Rising population and income are partial explanations, but the growth of traffic also reflects today's complex systems of production, which involve many plants and often many countries, all participating in an integrated production process. A look at the volume and variety of goods and materials movement in the United States provides a measure of the resources needed to maintain logistical support for an industrial society. It also measures the magnitude of the transportation investments required in low-income countries attempting to improve their economic condition through industrial growth.

Table Six / U.S. Economic Trends and Transportation (Indexes with 1972 = 100)

Year	GNP (in 1972 dollars)	Industrial Production	Population	Intercity Ton-miles	Intercity Passenger-miles
1940	29	21	63	30	25
1950	45	38	72	51	39
1960	62	55	86	63	60
1970	92	90	98	93	91
1980	124	123	109	120	120
1985	141	139	114	117	140

Sources: Transportation Policy Associates, *Transportation in America*, 4th ed. (Washington, D.C., March 1986), p. 3.

Table Seven / How U.S. Intercity Freight Is Moved

	Millions of Tons	Percentage	Billions of Ton-miles	Percentage
Rail	1,522	27.8	935	37.5
Truck	2,096	38.3	605	24.2
Oil pipelines	917	16.8	568	22.7
Inland and coastal water	930	17.0	382	15.3
Air	5	0.1	7	0.3
Total	5,470	100.0	2,497	100.0

Sources: Transportation Policy Associates, *Transportation in America,* 3d ed. (Washington, D.C., November 1985), p. 6.

Producing a ton of steel in the United States requires the transportation of 1.3 tons of raw materials. Iron ore is the principal ingredient and has to be moved from Australia, Brazil, Venezuela, Sweden, India, and China. Giant vessels deliver as much as a quarter million tons of ore per trip from Brazil to Baltimore. The steel mills also require delivery of millions of tons of scrap iron, limestone, and oxygen. Once the steel is produced, it must be shipped to a host of industries, including the transportation sector, construction companies, and the producers of machinery and equipment. In the United States these three buyers require an average of 80 million tons a year, and once this tonnage is moved it will reappear on the transport system in the form of intermediate and finished goods.

Chemicals are also among the major bulk commodities moving on the industrial transportation system. Hundreds of materials produced by the chemical industries were nonexistent only a few years ago, but today

Table Eight / Countries with Major Dependence on Railroad Freight

Country	Railroad Freight, 1984 (Billions of Ton-miles)
U.S.S.R.	2,064
United States	805
China	342
Canada	136
India	88
Hungary	88
Poland	80
South Africa	59
Brazil	52
Romania	45
Czechoslovakia	44
France	42
Federal Republic of Germany	39
Democratic Republic of Germany	38
Japan	24
Percentage of world total	87
Total for fifteen countries	3,946
World total	4,544

Source: Bureau of the Census, *Statistical Abstract of the United States, 1982–1983* (Washington, D.C., 1982), pp. 880–81.

the output of the fifty top chemicals in the United States, from acetone to xylene, exceeds a quarter of a billion tons annually. A single big company such as Dupont concludes a million and a quarter freight transactions annually, using ten thousand different carriers to serve its nine hundred plants and their customers. The transportation of energy is also of critical importance. Energy resources in the form of solids, liquids, and gases supply the factories, power plants, households, and transport systems of industrial economies in volumes that account for one fourth of all the freight that moves in the world.

Coal supplies about a fifth of U.S. energy and has the most visible impact on the transportation system. It is mined in twenty-five states and transported to every state except Hawaii. Three out of four tons are delivered to electric utilities; the rest are delivered to coke plants and various manufacturing establishments. But in recent years new sources of energy and new methods of transport have alleviated the energy transport problem. With the development of seamless welded pipe, natural gas is now moving nationwide from thirty-four originating states to forty-four million homes. It is used not only for heating, cooling, and cooking but also for manufacturing iron and steel, clay, glass, paper, and fertilizer. A million miles of pipelines are now in service in the United States—up 50 percent since 1960.

An industrial society also moves great volumes of materials for buildings and other structures. In the United States, over four hundred thousand construction firms are normally engaged in these activities, which are about equally divided among residential structures, commercial developments, and nonbuilding construction such as transportation and utilities. A conventional single-family home requires the delivery of thirty thousand separate components from factories all over the country.[3]

Trucking is an integral part of the construction process, permitting closely scheduled arrival of materials as needed. Steel, lumber, roofing, doors, windows, and other components arrive as needed, eliminating the difficulties of on-site storage. Construction accounts for most of the billion tons of crushed stone and the 800 million tons of sand and gravel transported in the United States in a single year. Fifty-eight hundred companies deliver these materials to construction projects, and transport requirements have been increasing as local sources are depleted and supplies become farther removed from construction sites. The cost of transporting sand and gravel to asphalt and cement plants often exceeds the cost of the materials themselves.

Cement production requires the delivery of over one hundred million tons of raw materials a year, including limestone, clay, shale, sand, and gypsum. Manufacturers rely on rail and waterway transport about equally for moving supplies to distribution points, while cement destined for ultimate consumers moves mostly by truck. Plants are generally located within two hundred miles of the large population centers that compose the major markets, since it is generally uneconomical to transport this material longer distances overland. But if water transport is available, cement manufacturers may ship to distributing centers as far as one thousand miles away.[4] Recently ocean transport has become so efficient that foreign-made cement is being shipped into the United States from as far away as Asia and Australia. Spain sends cement to East Coast and Gulf ports, where ships take on return loads of coal to supply Spanish plants with the ingredients for producing more cement. Recent years have also witnessed a growing number of cement companies arriving from abroad, with some forty foreign-owned plants in the United States now manufacturing more than a fourth of the nation's total output.

While much of the freight traffic in an industrial economy is generated by the transportation of primary products, the final output of producer and consumer goods involves high-value commodities that need fast and flexible delivery. Trucks supply this type of intercity transport, much of it for overnight or second-day delivery. Thousands of trucks in the United States are also engaged in maintaining and installing telephones and electric service, as well as supplying water and gas. Groceries, bakeries, hotels, and resorts rely on truck fleets to keep them supplied, and construction companies, mining firms, and government bureaus all rely on truck fleets to conduct their daily operations. Twenty thousand establishments in the apparel industry depend on trucks to deliver clothing, often on racks ready to be hung in the store. Annual deliveries include billions of dresses, suits, stockings, socks, and shoes. If all the retail, wholesale, industrial, and service truck fleets of more than ten vehicles are added together, American businesses depend on more than five million motor vehicles to sustain their operations.

Millions of small parcels and documents are also handled by intermodal truck and airplane services in the United States. The privately owned United Parcel Service (UPS) moves six million packages a day, more than the U.S. Postal Service. UPS has 600,000 regular customers, who are served by a fleet of thirty-eight thousand vans recently augmented by a fleet of cargo aircraft. Overnight deliveries are made almost anywhere in the country, as well as in Europe.[5]

Time-sensitive shipments by Federal Express also play a major role in American business. Overnight shipments are flown to a single assembly point at the airport in Memphis, Tennessee. There the packages are sorted each night and moved to final destinations in fifteen thousand communities via the company's fleet of aircraft and trucks. Federal Express makes next-morning delivery throughout the United States with the help of thousands of computer terminals that handle requests and instruct drivers. Services have also been extended to Europe. A private communications satellite serves the system. Since a large part of the small package business consists of documents, the Federal Express telecommunications network now delivers facsimile copies in a matter of hours as an alternative to overnight transportation. International overnight delivery of time-sensitive materials is also provided to five continents by DHL and other worldwide courier services, and much of this could also be taken care of electronically.

Trucks are performing functions in the United States which have significant implications for the transportation future of developing countries, where the truck is often thought of only as an unwelcome competitor of the railroads. But most trucks in the United States play a very different role. Failure to understand this has led to restrictive measures against truck operations in many countries, denying industry the kind of supporting services that cannot be supplied by alternative rail or water transport.

Industrial Freight in the Third World

Industrial development is beginning to impose new burdens on the unprepared domestic transportation networks of Third World nations. In the middle-income developing countries only 23 percent of gross domestic product was accounted for by industry in 1960, but twenty-three years later the figure had nearly doubled. Similar data for low-income countries show the industrial sector growing from 17 to 34 percent.[6] The construction of steel, cement, and fertilizer plants and the development of mineral, forest, and energy resources are transforming many parts of the Third World which were almost entirely rural farm economies two decades ago.

To date the tonnage of materials needing to be transported in developing countries has been modest—on the order of only one thousand to two thousand ton-miles per capita per year, as compared to the six thousand to ten thousand ton-miles typical of industrial countries. The reasons are apparent. Rural people build their own houses with locally available materials such as mud, grass, and bamboo, and little use is made of the cement, timber, steel, brick, glass, and fixtures used in western countries. Even in the urban areas of the Third World, most people cannot afford conventional housing, and whole cities are constructed of scrap metals, wooden crates, burlap, and other scavenged materials. Much of the construction industry in developing countries, therefore, is independent of the transportation system.

Events are changing this picture as the move from rural areas to the cities swells the urban population and necessitates public-sector participation in the construction of shelter and community facilities. Municipal governments are supplying building sites and materials for self-help housing and are constructing sanitation systems, water supply networks, schools, streets, and other community facilities. The result is to multiply the tonnage of building materials to be transported, including stone, sand, cement, and lumber. There has also been a marked increase in the amount of low-income housing structures provided by governments to help meet the rising need for urban shelter, and these projects add substantially to the demand for transportation.

The United Nations estimates that the minimum world needs for shelter during the last quarter of the century will exceed a billion dwelling units. There is also a massive backlog of needed repairs to existing houses, and over half the world's population has no safe and reliable water supply or sewage disposal systems. A major effort to improve these conditions will result in very large increases in the movement of lumber, cement, steel, and other materials.

Energy sources have also had limited impact on transportation in most Third World countries to date. The commercial energy consumed in preindustrial societies in 1980 accounted for only 12 percent of the total commercial energy consumed in the world. In most low-income countries, a fourth to a third of all energy is still being derived from local supplies of wood and waste—cow dung, coconut shells, rice husks, and similar materials. Some kerosene is used for cooking on rainy days, but, for the most part, the rural family gets along with wood and waste materials picked up and carried to the home, and there has been relatively little transportation of commercial energy materials. (Per capita consumption of commercial energy in India, for example, is less than 2 percent of U.S. per capita consumption.)

This, too, is beginning to change, in part because close-by supplies of wood for fuel are disappearing, and the need for animal waste as fertilizer competes with its use as a fuel. Rural electrification is also under way on a large scale, and the generation of electricity is multiplying the need to transport coal, oil, and gas. Industrial expansion also increases the demand for power, and total consumption of commercial energy in the Third World is now increasing at a rate of 6 percent a year, faster than the growth of GNP.[7]

The transportation impact of global industrialization is thus only beginning to be felt as the growth of cities and the building of new manufacturing establishments create major new requirements for energy, construction, and raw materials. The most vulnerable parts of the system are the highways that involve the most costly requirements, and the trucking fleets that are generally far below the levels necessary to support efficient processes of production and to permit the conduct of retail trade and service activities.

Thailand, for example, is a middle-income country with a better than average transportation system, yet one that is proving to be quite inadequate to meet the pressing new needs that Thai industry is beginning to generate. Transport and communications account for about 25 percent of all Thai public investment and are the largest expenditure item in the development effort. Yet even this may be insufficient to meet industrial freight requirements, which may double in ten years. The overburdened Thai railroad system will be called upon to move heavy volumes of long-distance traffic, while already congested roads are expected to bear the principal burden of carrying manufactured goods and predominantly short-haul traffic. It is expected that trucks, which now account for 70 percent of the total, will move 90 percent of all Thai freight by 1990.

Growing reliance on motor transport will require accelerated road-building efforts both to upgrade the conditions of the main and provincial highways and to construct or improve some twenty-five thousand

Figure Eight / Headloading in the construction industry in India. World Bank photo by Ray Witlin.

to thirty-five thousand miles of local roads.[8] The latter facilities are necessary to further the development of agriculture and raise farm incomes to make it possible for the rural population to purchase the products of urban industry. The transportation requirements of industrialization in Thailand have also been magnified by the heavy concentration of population and production in Bangkok. The 5 million people living in Bangkok account for 10 percent of the nation's population and for 63 percent of its urban population. Approximately one out of four dollars of gross domestic product is accounted for by the Bangkok metropolitan area. Traffic conditions are among the worst in the world, and the city is troubled by poor sanitation and poor shelter, which compete for scarce resources. The cost of improving the area's transport facilities, including the port, highways, and mass transportation, have thus far been too great to permit anything like the investments that could bring the necessary relief. A vast program to disperse industrial development away from Bangkok to the east coast of the Gulf of Thailand may be part of the answer. Ports, airports, rail lines, and highway improvements are included in the new multibillion-dollar, urban-industrial complex that will shift heavy industry to the south. But clearly Thailand's industrial growth will require costly and sustained efforts to meet the minimum transportation needs of a rapidly changing economy.

Industrial development in India presents still greater problems. While the rail system has registered important gains in the movement of coal, steel, cement, and fertilizer, the poor roads and the lack of trucks have been major obstacles. Large inventories must be maintained by industries, to be sure of being supplied with vital materials, and the inability of the transport system to meet factory schedules often forces a slowdown of production.

On the national highway network in India, which is comprised of the nation's most heavily traveled routes, a large part of the system has only one lane. There are numerous missing links, and many river crossings lack bridges. The much larger mileage of state highways that are the major part of India's main road network is in far worse condition, and local roads throughout the country are often little better than animal trails and footpaths.

The supply of motor vehicles is far below what is needed to serve an industrial economy. There are approximately one million trucks and buses in all of India, as compared to twelve million in Japan. Production of commercial vehicles is less than fifty thousand a year. If all the trucks in India were to have an average life of ten years, it would take twice as many new units a year just to replace the fleet, without any additions to accommodate the growth of industry.

The great distances that separate India's natural resources from its major cities accentuate the task of supplying transport capacity for industry. It is over one thousand miles from Bombay to Calcutta, or Bombay to Delhi; and about fifteen hundred miles from Delhi to Madras. Coal, which is the single largest item of traffic on the railways, has to move all the way across the country from the Bengal-Bihar district in the east to Bombay on the west coast, where a third of India's manufacturing is concentrated. Most raw materials for the steel, cement, energy, and chemical industries move by rail, aided to some degree by coastal shipping and to a limited extent by road transport. But there are many instances of long delays and uncertain scheduling that create costly problems for industry. In addition, much of the nation's rich natural resources remain untapped because of poor transport. One-fifth of the country is forest and contains a rich variety of hard- and softwood, but in many areas there is still no way to harvest the wood and move it to production sites. India has one-fourth of the world's iron ore and enough coal to last for over a century, yet these and other resources often cannot be used due to poor access and the high costs of transport.

In the past two decades, substantial efforts have been made to modernize the Indian transport system. One-fifth to one-fourth of all public investment has been for transport. About two-thirds of this investment has been for railroads, which still account for two-thirds of all the nation's freight movement. In recent years, however, outlays for rail facilities have declined to about one-third of public investment in transport, and greater emphasis has been given to roads.

The growth of the Indian economy since 1950 has been substantial, and the transport system has accommodated a large expansion of heavy industry and has been able to supply the basic needs of an additional 300 million people. But an average income of $260 per capita in 1984 measures how far the economy falls short of requirements and how much greater the transport system's capacity must be to accommodate further industrial growth. The government of India expects a doubling of rail freight between the late seventies and the early nineties, and more than a tripling of goods movement by road. But road transport estimates are not realistic, according to the Indian Planning Commission, since they would require an average net addition to the truck fleet of five times as many trucks a year as are now being provided. Even the rail tonnage projections may be impractical unless sufficient short-haul and less-than-carload traffic is able to shift from rail to road, thus freeing the rails for the movement of heavy commodities over long distances.

Shortages in rail freight facilities may also occur if the nearly four-fold increase in rail passenger service is realized. About half of all train movements in India serve passengers, but only 35 percent of rail revenues are derived from this source. Lower passenger fares are made possible by subsidies from freight, and the result has been to encourage still more travel and to reduce freight capacity. Intercity bus transport and aviation are now assuming a larger part of the passenger load, but far more of these passenger facilities will be needed if the rail system is to meet industrial freight requirements.

Improvement in Indian railway freight performance in recent years indicates that long waiting times have been reduced and that the delivery of coal, cement, and other commodities has shown marked improvement. Financial results remain unsatisfactory, however, due in part to losses from passenger services, uneconomic branch lines, and socially dictated low rates on the movement of food grains, salt, firewood, and other items. These subsidies to consumers, along with overstaffing, add considerably to the cost of railway operations. The overall result is that rail revenues are able to cover only about two-fifths of the capital investment needed to keep pace with further growth of the economy. Government subsidies must make up the difference.

Policies affecting truck transport are the opposite—restrictive rather than supportive. National permits limit the number of trucks that can operate in interstate services, and each state charges its own fees. Local octroi posts operated by local governments require trucks entering the city to pay a tax on what is carried, ranging from a few cents for a truckload of sand to perhaps $50 for a truck carrying furniture. It is estimated that delays at those posts absorb a fourth of the total running time between cities. Although local governments maintain that they need these revenues, collection costs take most of the proceeds, and several states have abandoned the practice.

Other obstacles to trucking include the waiting time involved in purchasing a vehicle, which is often several years. During that time a sizeable deposit is required, which many operators cannot afford. Additional problems arise from the poor condition of Indian roads. Roads designed to last five years are being destroyed by overloaded trucks and are not being repaired and upgraded at the end of their design life, while road funds made available to the states for keeping the national highways in adequate repair are frequently used for other purposes.

These and other frustrating conditions appear to be the result of a conviction that long-distance hauling by road will spell the end of the railways. But the future of the railways lies not in moving furniture or cattle or farm produce but in carrying more efficiently the very large volumes of heavy bulk commodities that can be moved no other way. Performing that task alone is an enormous challenge in the world's seventh largest industrial nation, which by the end of this century will be attempting to supply the material needs of 1 billion people.[9]

The transportation problems facing China in a period of rapid industrialization are in some ways comparable to those of the Indian subcontinent. China is equally dependent on the railways for freight movement, and some two-thirds of all that is carried moves by rail. Chinese rail traffic is the third highest in the world. But inadequate roads and the small size and inefficient performance of the truck fleet pose serious problems of keeping pace with the freight requirements of rapidly expanding industries, including light industry that is highly dependent on road transport for fast service and flexible schedules.

In the coming years the Chinese railways, already the third largest rail freight carriers in the world, will have all the work they can possibly handle in moving the nation's coal, timber, cement, steel, fertilizer, and other heavy bulk commodities. Water transport and pipelines will be needed to supplement rail capacity. But for the parallel increases in manufactured goods movement, greater use of trucks and extensive improvement of highways will be the major means of supplying new industries with the closely integrated transport services needed in the production and marketing of high-value goods. The situation is comparable to that of Japan in the mid-fifties, when it became apparent that small and inefficient trucks operating on obsolete roads provided no basis for a manufacturing sector that could compete in world markets. The bold strokes that remedied the Japanese transport bottleneck included the building of major arterial highways to limited-access expressway standards, with financing made possible by tolls and taxes on motor fuel. In addition, the automotive industry produced trucks with the capacity and performance necessary to match the high quality of the roads. China's industrial sector will be in jeopardy until a physical and financial strategy can be put in place that will relieve the railways of the small shipments and short hauls that should be moving by road, and that will supply modern industrial plants with the closely tailored truck delivery services that must become an integral part of the processes of production.[10]

The transportation systems of developing countries vary in the degree to which they fall short of the capacity and quality called for by their industrial development plans and potentials. Bringing transport performance to reasonably tolerable levels will be costly and time-consuming, but the effort could be aided, and unnecessary problems avoided, by observation of current and past experience in developed countries. The mistakes in financing, organization, regulation, and rate-making which had unfortunate consequences elsewhere need not be repeated. It should be possible from that experience to apply the more effective concepts and newer technologies of recent years, and to avoid some of the costs and inefficiencies that have plagued the freight systems of nations that industrialized in an earlier period, when a wider choice of technologies was not available.

Improving Freight Performance

The possibilities of supplying greater freight-carrying capacity in developing countries have been augmented as the United States and other industrial countries continue to develop new technology and innovative concepts. Many of these advances have already had important spillover effects in Third World countries, and others provide a demonstration of how it may be possible to establish more economical services as developing country systems are expanded.

Automatic loading and unloading equipment on vessels and in ports is now reducing ship turnaround times and alleviating port congestion in developing countries. The use of containers has made substantial contributions to cargo-carrying performance by reducing pilferage, paper work, and the time required for loading and unloading. In marine transport, a supertanker of a half-million deadweight tons operates with fewer hands than Columbus needed to sail the *Santa Maria*. Unit trains that shuttle huge volumes of coal, wheat, and other bulk commodities between a single origin and one destination have also stretched rail freight-carrying capacity.

Containers and computers, combined with deregulation, are helping to avoid the waste that results from operating each method of transportation separately. Recent growth of rail-highway and sea-land container services, as well as of overnight air-truck express, indicates the potentials of intermodal delivery under a single management. In the United States, rail cars carry truck trailers in a piggyback service on short-length trains that operate on frequent schedules to supply multiple round trips daily between principal cities. On very long hauls, such as Asia to Europe, the container has made it possible to combine ocean transport with overland routes or "land bridges" that cut the time and cost of international deliveries. One around-the-world container line now has the capacity to carry ninety thousand containers at a time.

Progress toward intermodal freight transport has been made in a growing segment of the cargo business. Integrated rail-truck hauling services have been introduced by companies such as the CSX Corporation, which recently became the largest provider of "one-stop shipping." Studies by the U.S. Department of Transportation indicate that

Figure Nine / The unit train: one out of every five U.S. rail cars carries coal. Association of American Railroads photo.

an integrated road-rail system for the United States might permit a very substantial reduction in rail mileage, from the present 180,000 miles to a national network of some 25,000 miles of guideways for high-speed container services. The system might be built parallel to the Interstate Highway System, bypassing rail assembly yards and providing frequent scheduling of short trains moving at speeds of 85 to 120 miles per hour. Feeder truck lines serving some 160 intermodal terminals could supply service to 80 percent of the nation's metropolitan areas. The majority of all origins and destinations in the country would be located within 20 miles of a terminal.

Developing countries could benefit in many ways by similar types of intermodal freight systems. Railroads often attempt to retain the movement of small shipments and short-haul traffic that ought to be carried by truck, whereas trucks, because of their superior speed and flexibility, divert much of the available high-value traffic from the rails and add to railway deficits. Financial difficulties and wasteful competition could be overcome by integrated companies that offer a complete service by whatever method or combination of methods suits the need. The effect would be faster and more economical service, more profitable operations, and less resistance to new technology on the part of individual transport methods that are now competing rather than cooperating.

In some countries part of the solution for overburdened surface transport may be the use of pipelines for solids as well as liquids and gases. Automatic and continuous movement by pipeline can greatly reduce the problems of operating a transport system. Just as developed countries no longer count the movement of water and waste as transportation, the movement of petroleum and gas by pipelines has taken care of much of the energy deliveries that once dominated surface transport. Now it can be anticipated that coal, iron ore, chemicals, and other bulk commodities may follow the same course, going underground and being largely forgotten as part of the transport problem.

The separation of passenger from freight services may also increase transport capabilities. In some countries a doubling or tripling of rail freight capacity may be possible by eliminating conventional passenger services and shifting this traffic to a limited system designed exclusively for moving people. The heavy railway passenger traffic in many developing countries suggests that innovations in this area and greater reliance on bus and air transport may be especially helpful as a means of relieving overburdened freight-carrying facilities.

Developing countries with poor surface transport have demonstrated the benefits of air travel, and industrial shippers are depending heavily on air cargo movements. The growing reliance on air cargo is indicated by the fact that at the Port of New York and New Jersey the value of international air-borne commodities exceeds the value of ocean-borne general cargo. Among the ten top classes of air freight exports are office equipment, machinery, scientific instruments, aircraft, and aircraft parts. Air cargo arriving from other parts of the world includes clothing, footwear, machinery, electronic equipment, electric motors, and generators. This fast-growing interchange of industrial products, promoted by the speed and economy of intercontinental jet cargo liners, is supported by fast truck transportation.

The economic potentials of air cargo are measured by the international trading of the world's landlocked countries. Some landlocked West African cities are six hundred miles or more from the nearest transit port. The people of Rwanda, Niger, and Chad must cover distances of up to one thousand miles through neighboring countries to connect with the world transport system. And in Asia, goods moving to and from Nepal have five hundred miles of Indian territory to traverse between Katmandu and Calcutta, the nearest port.[11] These countries depend increasingly on air cargo operations to avoid poor surface transport and long delays in ports. The problems of landlocked countries have become critical in a world in which the success of many consumer industries depends to an increasing extent on filling orders promptly and keeping inventories low.

Third World countries have considerable opportunity, therefore, to depart from the organizational, financial, and technological paths taken at an earlier stage by the now industrialized nations. An important element in their strategy should be the organizing of transportation companies that make use of all methods of movement, aided by containerization. This approach would substitute for the rivalries that now exist between road and rail in particular, and that have often resulted in the preservation of uneconomic rail services and in the prevention of the growth of road transport by truck.

It is also possible that much of the heavy freight typical of goods traffic in developed countries might be avoided by changes in energy sources, urban growth policies, industrial location, and the basing of rates and fares on appropriate cost considerations. These and other aspects of Third World transport strategies will be discussed in chapters four and five.

The high cost of moving freight and the lack of reliable delivery over much of the global system are obvious barriers to industry and trade. But the inability of workers and entrepreneurs to travel with relative economy and convenience is also an impediment that limits levels of production and prevents successful marketing. Personal mobility may be no less significant than freight transportation in building an industrial nation. Chapter four addresses the mounting transportation problems of cities resulting from the growth of the urban-industrial sector, and the special difficulties of commuting between home and work.

Four / Cities in the Global Network

If the global transportation network should some day grind to a halt, the stoppage will take place in the world's great cities. Transportation facilities in cities are a small fraction of the global system, but they are vital links in the network. Cities are the origins, destinations, and transfer points for much of the world's freight and passenger movements, and local urban transport services support 40 percent of the earth's people and most of its industry. Cities are also the terminals for the intercontinental transport networks, the ports for twenty-two thousand ocean-going ships with their half a billion tons of cargo capacity, and the points of convergence for the world's rail and highway networks. Cities also provide three thousand major airports, where the world's commercial airliners board and disembark close to 1 billion passengers a year.

But urban systems threaten to become weak links in the chain. Metropolitan cities clogged with traffic suffer delays and poor service, which raise the cost of everything that is produced and consumed. The result is often a reduction in the competitive position of urban centers and in the quality of life for those who must put up with transport-induced noise, smog, discomfort, and inconvenience. The growth of population, industrialization, and urbanization threatens to worsen the congestion that has already reached ominous levels.

The cities and suburbs of the world have nevertheless been able to carry on their activities to date without serious disruption. Somehow the complex delivery systems keep working with minimum delay and inconvenience. These accomplishments are more remarkable when one considers the speed with which urban growth has taken place. As recently as 1950 there were only six cities in the world with a population of over 5 million, housing 47 million people. Recently there were twenty-six of those giant metropolitan areas, with a total population of 252 million.[1]

Approximately 40 percent of the world's population lives in cities, and in the year 2000 the figure will probably be over 50 percent. Altogether, the number of people living in urban settlements with a population of 20,000 or over is expected to increase to 2.2 billion by the year 2000, which is two and a half times the 1975 level.

This tremendous concentration of people and economic activity is contained in about 0.5 percent of the world's land area. (The rest of the earth's surface is forest, farms, cropland, wasteland, or parks and unused

Table Nine / Urbanization and per Capita Income

	GNP per Capita, 1984	Percentage of Population Urbanized, 1984
Low-income countries	$ 270	21
Middle-income countries	1,500	45
Industrialized countries	11,120	78

Source: World Bank, World Bank Development Report, 1983 (Washington, D.C., 1986), pp. 180–81, 240–41.

reservations.) In this small area are the highest costs of transportation, the greatest congestion, and the major need for investments to keep the transport system operating. The advantages of such concentration have become increasingly questionable in a world of vast land areas that are not being effectively used and that transportation and communications could be making accessible and useful.

The Rising Tide of Traffic

The city, Lewis Mumford once observed, sits like a spider in the midst of its transportation web. In Chicago, the web surrounding America's third largest metropolis serves the ingoing and outgoing shipments of fourteen thousand manufacturing plants, thirteen thousand wholesale establishments, and fifty-seven thousand retail outlets. Total outbound freight in a single year exceeds fifty million tons of everything from office furniture, soap, and sausages to railroad cars, envelopes, and barrels. Chicago is a port of call for fourteen overseas shipping lines, which move locally manufactured products to forty-seven ports in twenty-four countries.

On the local scene, the transit system and a network of expressways and commuter trains transport some 2 million workers to the job and back every day, while 300,000 trucks and a labyrinth of railroads keep the city supplied with a never-ending replenishment of meats and poultry, fish and vegetables, and millions of tons of other food that provide three meals a day for 8 million people. At O'Hare International, the world's busiest airport, 40 million people a year travel by plane.

Metropolitan Los Angeles provides life-support mobility for 11 million people, including 3 million employees who make the daily trek to work. There are four million motor vehicles and five hundred miles of freeways. The Los Angeles–Long Beach Harbor has forty-six miles of commercial waterfront, where five thousand ships handle sixty million tons of cargo annually, and transcontinental rail lines move everything from automobiles and chemicals to seafood and aerospace hardware.

Truck transportation in U.S. cities shows the important role of service vehicles in the total picture. One day's activity indicates that over 40 percent of truck operation involves the maintenance of utilities or the collection of rubbish. Thirty percent is for moving food and beverages, while energy supply and construction activities also account for substantial amounts of trucking. But the most impressive achievement of the world's urban transport systems is their capacity to deliver hundreds of millions of people to their jobs, and to repeat the process day after day with only occasional disruption of services. The costs and inconveniences of commuting represent an enormous use of time and other resources, and the bill for getting people to their jobs is a substantial item in municipal and household budgets. Although many cities have made substantial improvements in commuter facilities in recent years, the "rush hour" continues to cover more hours, more miles, and more vehicles, with no end in sight.

In the United States, the Interstate Highway System connecting the cities, as well as the extensions and beltways around them, is already severely overloaded. Many commuter routes are backed up for miles in the morning and evening rush hours. Growth of the suburbs continues to create new areas of traffic congestion on the fringes of metropolitan areas and in the vicinity of suburbia's giant shopping centers. The trend continues with increasing income, leisure time, and the growth of motor-vehicle ownership by three to four million units a year.

The extraordinary congestion of commuter facilities in big cities not only tries the patience of travelers but also reduces the living environment of those who lack the means of travel. Difficulties in moving around restrict job opportunities and make it difficult for low-income families to gain access to educational and recreational opportunities, as well as to medical and other services offered by the community. In many large U.S. cities—Chicago, Philadelphia, Baltimore, Washington, and Boston—20 percent or more of all households are carless. While the number of cars is growing, many of these additions are second and third cars, and carless households continue to confront special difficulties in a predominantly automotive society, where dispersal makes it difficult to travel by public transit.

In Third World countries, the cities and suburbs that suffer a far more serious lack of transportation pose life-threatening problems for the poor. Many people, when asked to name the most critical problem in their household, answer "transportation." What they mean is that transportation is necessary for getting a job, earning income, and getting enough to eat. Outlying slums and squatter settlements contain practically no jobs, so that survival depends on making a trip into the city to find work. People fortunate enough to have work in the city must depend on packed trains and buses, which are totally inadequate and are a burdensome daily expense for low-income riders.

The cost of improving urban transport is a heavy drain on municipal funds needed for other basic services, as illustrated by the situation in São Paulo, Brazil. In this metropolis of 10 million people (16 million by the end of the century), one-fourth of the population lives in poverty in *favelas* surrounding the city. The primary need is jobs, and jobs depend not only on transportation but also on education and health. The latter depends on pure water and adequate sanitation. São Paulo *favelas* are lacking in all these categories. Only 60 percent of São Paulo houses have a sewer connection, and only 40 percent have piped water. Yet in the late seventies the city's long-term plan was to spend five times more for transportation than for overcoming water and sewer deficiencies. Constructing a new subway, improving commuter rail service, and building an expressway around the city involve billions of dollars of construction and operating costs, while other living conditions continue to worsen and 450,000 people are added to the overcrowded city every year.

The future of urban transportation in rich and poor countries poses a universal dilemma. Transportation has made the metropolis possible, and the metropolis has made major contributions to human progress, but transportation difficulties are making conditions in many metropolitan areas intolerable. Cities that serve as the focal points for industry and trade need better transportation, but they need other services as well if they are to compete successfully in global markets.

Managing Mobility

The strategy of an increasing number of cities around the world is to deal with urban traffic not simply by building more roads and rapid transit but also by exerting an influence on demand and making more effective use of the transport facilities and equipment already available.

In the United States, governments and the private sector are seeking such relief through programs of transportation system management (TSM) aimed at making better use of existing investments in streets, transit, and other facilities. The idea of TSM is to view all elements of urban transportation, public and private, as parts of a single system organized and operated with appropriate traffic regulations and pricing policies. In theory, the approach would be to combine the pricing of automobile use and parking with preferential use of the streets by mass transit, and controls over automobile use during rush hours.[2]

Figure Ten / A commuter highway into Washington, D.C.; buses and car pools use exclusive lanes. U.S. Department of Transportation photo.

Much can be accomplished by measures designed to make more effective use of existing facilities. A number of cities, from Stockholm to Singapore, have introduced an effective combination of these measures. But on a global basis relatively little is being done. For example, most cities are allocating road and street space in inverse relation to efficiency. The automobile, which may carry the smallest percentage of traffic, gets most of the space; the bus, which carries a high proportion of traffic, gets relatively little space; and pedestrians, often the largest part of the traffic, usually get the least consideration. Pedestrian streets and exclusive roadways for buses are among the innovations that can bring about a more equitable solution.

Officials of Gothenberg, Sweden, have reallocated street space to favor pedestrians and public transport by a plan for rerouting automobiles in the downtown area. The central business district was divided into pie-shaped zones, and direct movement between zones by automobiles was prohibited. Cars are able to move from one zone to another only by traveling out to the peripheral ring road, using the appropriate radial to leave and reenter the desired zone. Within each zone, automobile movement is permitted without restriction. Public transit vehicles are allowed to move directly from one zone to another. Parking policies are part of the strategy, with hourly parking fees in the downtown area doubled, and maximum parking time restricted to two hours. Automobile traffic on major downtown streets has been cut in half.

In Bologna, Italy, a system-wide traffic strategy demonstrates how a comprehensive effort has upgraded the environment, increased travel speeds, and reduced accidents. The program reduced auto use by forty thousand vehicles a day, or 20 percent, and increased transit patronage by 50 percent.[3] The strategy in Bologna is city-wide, including the suburbs as well as the historic center, because much of the traffic that clogs the center originates in the outlying neighborhoods. All streets were classified as either primary or secondary. Various physical measures, such as closing intersections and side streets, have made primary routes more suitable for through traffic. The secondary systems have been restricted to those who live in the neighborhood or have reason to be there. Transit has been made more competitive with the automobile, thanks to all-bus lanes, one-way streets, the designation of bypass routes around the center, and the elimination of bus fares in rush hours. Exclusive contraflow bus lanes have helped in making trip time by public transit comparable to time by car. The combination of time savings and free transit has reduced the number of cars using the primary system in commuting hours and has enhanced the safety, quiet, and visual quality of neighborhoods.

Hundreds of cities around the world have created "auto-restricted zones" in downtown areas, where the automobile operates so inefficiently that converting selected streets to pedestrian or bicycle use is little loss for the motorist and often a boon to pedestrians and merchants. European cities, from Amsterdam and Cologne to Barcelona and Munich, demonstrate the advantages of this approach to urban mobility. Cities in developing countries have far greater need to provide such facilities for people who walk or ride bicycles to work. The percentage of total trips made on foot is substantial in cities such as Dar-es-Salaam, Taipei, Madras, Seoul, and Bogotá. Surveys suggest that over half of all trips taken by the poorest families are on foot. The bicycle also plays an important role in many cities and needs special pathways. In a selected group of twenty-two countries keeping records, there were forty million motorized two-wheelers on the registration lists in the seventies, and an estimated two to four times as many bicycles.[4]

Charging automobile drivers the extra costs incurred by the city to furnish them with street capacity during hours of heavy traffic is one way to bring about a more equitable use of street space. The government of Singapore was the first to adopt such a policy, which requires the purchase of a special license for cars entering the downtown area

Figure Eleven / Rickshaw transportation in Bangladesh. World Bank photo by Tomas Sennett.

with fewer than four passengers. Hong Kong has tested the further possibility of pricing the use of automobiles by installing sensors in the pavement to detect the time and frequency of trips into congested central areas. Vehicle identification numbers can be recorded electronically and transmitted to a central computer, where each car is assessed for the specific uses made of the street system. If the tests are successful, motorists can then be billed for street costs incurred during the month in the same way that consumers are charged for electricity, water, or telephone.

Private financing of urban transport is another means of helping to defray the high costs incurred by municipalities. Industries, government agencies, universities, and other groups are participating in this so-called "privatization" of collective transportation, using various forms of paratransit such as taxis, vans, and dial-a-bus systems. In a seven-county area around Detroit, 109 organizations provide their own bus service for the handicapped, the elderly, and other special groups. Private interests operate more vehicles than the Detroit transit system.

Paratransit is also a major recourse for hard-pressed commuters in Third World cities. The jitney taxi or public automobile that carries 4 to 8 or more passengers provides a ride equivalent in many ways to that of a private automobile. The ride is faster than that by bus, there is almost no wait, everyone sits, and there is no way to overload with standees. Large fleets and numerous routings make possible nearly door-to-door service. In Manila, thousands of jeepneys have become the principal means of public transport, and the same is true of the *por puestos* in Caracas and the *peseros* in Mexico City. The fare is higher than regular transit but much lower than conventional taxis. In most cities that operate these public automobiles, there is almost always a vehicle in sight, eliminating much of the waiting time that frustrates patrons of conventional transit.

Extending Public Transit

In most big cities, strategies to improve transportation now include the construction of rail rapid transit, much of it underground. In 1980 some thirty cities were constructing new subways or extensions of existing lines. There are between sixty and seventy cities with so-called metros or subways, and they carry an estimated 12 billion passengers a year.[5] Half the total of some twenty-one hundred miles of line are located in a few very large cities: New York, Tokyo, Moscow, Paris, London, Washington, San Francisco, and Berlin. Cities in less developed countries that have undertaken major metro construction include Seoul, Rio de Janeiro, São Paulo, Mexico City, Caracas, and Hong Kong.

The number of cities that typically could qualify for a metro is in-

Figure Twelve / The automobile comes to Singapore. World Bank photo by Edwin Huffman.

creasing. There are 21 cities in the world with 5 million or more people each, and the number of such concentrations may be nearly three times as great by the end of the century. Forty of these cities will be in developing countries, and only 12 have built metros thus far. Another 133 cities will have between 2 million and 5 million people, of which only 20 have rapid transit systems already operating. By the end of the century, the length of the world's rapid transit routes may have increased to about four thousand miles. However, due to high capital and operating costs, developing countries with most of the problems may have only a sixth of the mileage.[6] Some cities, such as Singapore and Hong Kong, are ideally situated to benefit from rapid transit, because they have clearly delineated traffic routes and well-defined limits to the urbanized area. Where physical conditions are favorable, innovative financing may also be possible. In Singapore the construction costs of the new subway can be paid for by the sale or lease of publicly owned land at the station stops, and prevention of excessive surface traffic has already been arranged through the special licensing of automobiles.

In 1983 Caracas also opened its new air-conditioned subway, which, is designed to counter the immense traffic jams that have made the Venezuelan capital extremely difficult to move around in. But as in other cities of both the developed and the developing countries, the cost of building and operating a rapid transit system makes it increasingly difficult to allocate sufficient funds for this purpose and at the same time finance water and sanitation facilities, health and education costs, and other services. In Caracas the modern rapid-transit line passes the hillside shanty towns, where the city's poor live in makeshift housing that lacks water supply or garbage collection; these other needs will remain unmet if transportation deficits result in further pressure on the public treasury. A similar problem may be confronting the United States, where housing and blighted neighborhoods remain substandard while cities paying for better transportation have little left for improving their living conditions.

In many instances, underground rail rapid transit may not promise the best solution to the growing congestion of the big city. The answer depends on the kind of city and on whether it is willing to control the density of development and the uses of land. Otherwise, the feedback effects of rapid transit may be ever-higher concentration of offices, displacement of residential neighborhoods, more commuter travel, and greater congestion than before the metro was built.

Other factors limit the benefits of rapid transit. High cost per mile means that mileage has to be limited despite the large urbanized area to be served. Routes also have to be restricted to those on which traffic densities are high enough to support the service. This means that good bus transportation will continue to be essential, both as a feeder service to the subway and as a supplementary system. As cities grow, good bus transport may eventually require a network of exclusive streets for buses. It may be wise to establish such a bus system before building a subway, to determine whether this would suffice without a heavy commitment of resources to underground rapid transit. What is saved could then be used for housing and needed community services.

A conventional bus trip costs only one-third as much as a trip by automobile or rapid transit. But a rapid-transit strategy might still be economical from the standpoint of the total urban activity system if it supports patterns of development that produce savings in the cost of other services (water, sewer, fire protection). If this should be the case, rapid transit could be financed by recouping part of the incremental real estate values resulting from the subway investment. Riders should not be obliged to pay the total bill when much of the profit from subway operation accrues to the owners of urban land.

Politically, a subway is a monumental achievement as well as an impressive means of transport for those in a position to use it. However, in many cities riders will remain a small percentage of total travelers. The poorest families may not be able to pay the metro fare, and their trips are generally short and not well-served by subway. The increased capacity

of rapid transit may also encourage so much new development in surrounding areas that both surface streets and underground rail facilities
will become heavily overcrowded. Avoiding this result calls for strict
land-use controls and the encouragement of mixed-use development
around station stops to provide a combination of jobs and housing that
reduces travel and avoids having most commuters heading in one direction.

Mobility and Urban Design

As urban concentrations continue to grow in size, the idea that urban
transport problems can be solved by greater transport capacity often
turns out to be an illusion. Additional facilities generate new travel
demand which quickly absorbs whatever capacity is available. Expanding transport capacity will not overcome urban traffic congestion without more satisfactory community design aimed at rearranging land use
and combining better planned cities with pricing policies and other measures aimed at reducing unmanageable demands on the system.

The difficulties stem from the nature of cities. The city was originally
the major means of communication. It performed this function by locating activities close together to make personal contact easy. The automobile, however, has provided a new means of communication that over-
comes distance but requires excessive amounts of urban land. It also
promotes dispersal and low density, which have greatly increased the
dimensions of urban areas and made it more difficult to supply public
transportation. The result has been a blow to the carless, who must
operate in an environment that depends on the automobile and who
must rely on public transport, which may be inaccessible, inadequate, or
nonexistent. As a result, big-city residents may find all methods of
transportation—walking, driving, and public transit—unsatisfactory.

Mobility and lack of mobility have had a governing influence on the
size and shape of cities. In earlier times, this influence was largely due to
constraints imposed by poor transport. Poor transport contributed to
overcrowding, lack of open space, and urban blight. Later, with the
greater capacity of automotive transport in particular, the cities grew in
population and in geographic expanse. But in the process, mobility was
used as a means of escaping the disorder by moving out into the suburbs.
But the typical suburb is only a partial community that requires daily
transportation to distant work places, shops, and services. The result is
an increasing demand for transportation and an ever-larger dedication
of resources for mobility, to the neglect of many other pressing urban
needs.

Urban design, however, can produce a more satisfying environment, bringing jobs closer to the household, and households closer to shops, schools, and recreation. The approach to building better communities is a compromise between mobility and accessibility. While it is still possible to travel long distances from home to work, or from home to shopping and recreation, it is also feasible to do all these things close to home.

It has been correctly pointed out that the separation of homes from work places is in many ways desirable and necessary—desirable because a certain amount of isolation between the workday and the affairs of the household may be psychologically helpful. People who once lived over the family store or in the company town are not anxious to bring housing and work place closer together.[7] In any case, separation is often necessary because of the large scale of many economic activities, the need for an establishment to be in a particular location, or the need to locate away from a residential area. In addition, one family member may be situated close to the job, while another working member may have to travel many miles in the opposite direction.

The point, however, is that people should have a choice of how much spatial separation they will have to live with. The conventional city has so compartmentalized urban life and neglected the environment that perpetual motion has become obligatory. It is no longer true, however, that offices have to be close together for interaction or that the working place creates a poor environment that requires separation from residential areas. Communications provide the means of close interaction, and the well-designed city has shown that industries can make good neighbors and that attractive environments can reduce the need for escape.

A well-arranged community can reduce the length of the work trip for those who wish to take advantage of the possibility. It locates a variety of daily needs close at hand, extends the possibility of making short trips on foot or on bicycle, and increases safety by separating people from motorized traffic. The motor vehicle in turn is made more compatible with the community by the provision of exclusive motorways, off-street parking, and the removal of conflicts with pedestrians. For public transport, the provision of exclusive rights-of-way can make the standard of service more comparable to that of the automobile.

Substantial progress in urban design is now being made in many parts of the world, and transportation is becoming the means of improving the environment rather than destroying it. Streets are being converted to new uses, waterfronts are being restored, highways landscaped, and roadways turned over to pedestrians. Waterfronts, piers, and warehouses are becoming restaurants and condominiums, and railroad yards are the downtown sites for the new town in-town, with its hotels, offices, apartments, and shopping arcades.

In the United States, the use of obsolete transport facilities as sites for redevelopment began in Philadelphia, when Penn Center was built over the tracks and yards of the Pennsylvania Railroad. Boston's Prudential Center was made possible by using the Boston and Albany railroad yards in Back Bay. Later the unused piers and warehouses along the harbor became restaurants and condominiums, followed by the vacating of streets to provide the pedestrian setting for Boston's City Hall and Faneuil Hall Market. Eventual removal of the elevated highway, which robs the area of light and creates a barrier against the sea, would make the land beneath the central artery and adjacent properties available for housing on what is one of the country's most desirable harbor fronts. A combination of townhouses, apartments, shops, parks, and marinas would enable Bostonians to live and enjoy recreation within a short walking distance of downtown offices, making urban life more attractive and economic activities more productive.

Transportation has been a major element in the renewal of downtown Baltimore. The entire Inner Harbor was once an environmental nightmare. Railroads and rail yards completely enveloped the city center, and warehouses erected along the waterfront eliminated any opportunities for housing or recreation. Expressways formed a web of entanglements and maintained the dominance of mobility as an unwanted shaper of urban form. With the coming of the automobile age, those residents able to escape made off for the suburbs. But the Charles Center redevelopment began the process of downtown renewal, and development of the Inner Harbor, with its variety of restaurants, shops, and other attractions, became the city's major feature.

What made it all possible was the diverting of a proposed expressway and the elimination of a harbor bridge, clearing the way for a downtown facing open water. The mobility system incorporated into the plan was a further key to success. It included a boulevard link to the central business district, a pedestrian promenade, and the reuse of rail yards, streets, and docks. The land released by the elimination of obsolete transport facilities made way for the Convention Center, housing, neighborhood shops, and modern office buildings.

New York is also using obsolete transportation facilities to create a new downtown area that brings housing within closer range of jobs in Lower Manhattan's office district. Battery Park City, a new town intown, is being built on a landfill along the Hudson River, opposite the World Trade Center. It will provide ninety-two acres of a mixed development, with some sixteen thousand housing units as well as offices and retail shops to meet the needs of the resident population. Thirty percent of the land will be left vacant, and there will be waterfront pedestrian ways with spectacular views of the harbor and the Statue of Liberty. The basic objective is to provide attractive living close to the concentration of offices, making possible a close-in community that is alive both day and night and that allows easy commuting for its residents.

Transportation plays a vital role in Battery Park City. The landfill operation removed the derelict piers that covered the Hudson waterfront, substituting pedestrian walkways. The streets are designed to take advantage of natural vistas and to discourage through traffic. The projected work force, as many as 35,000 people, will have access to public transit through an overhead pedestrian walkway to the World Trade Center, while park-lined boulevards and landscaped streets will supply the amenities that neighborhoods in a densely populated area need. The Battery Park City Authority has used the street and transportation plan as the framework of the new town, leaving to individual developers the task of fitting housing and shops and other commercial development into the places reserved for them. This type of predesigned urbanization is now taking place in new growth areas outside the cities, to help decongest existing urban concentrations and to create the multi-centered urban regions of the future.

Guiding Urban Growth

Earlier centuries were able to cope with urban problems because population growth and technological changes were not great enough to demand a quick response. Balance in the system was accomplished by a continuing process of relatively minor adjustment. Today the changes affecting urban areas are massive and relentless. Improvisation is not enough, and a process of consciously designing multi-purpose and partially self-contained communities on a region-wide scale has become an increasingly attractive alternative to spontaneous urbanization. Such developments can be of governing importance to the future of urban development as a new breed of city builder emerges and begins putting the concept of total urban systems into practice.

An early plea for such an approach was made before the turn of the century by Ebenezer Howard, who expressed dismay at the living conditions endured in Britain's industrial cities, where millions lived in squalor.[8] The remedy he prescribed was to stem the tidal wave of population crowding into the cities by countering the attractions of the old city with sufficient attractions elsewhere. By so doing it would be possible not only to provide for growth but also to redesign the old cities for fewer people, who could be provided with a healthier and more humane environment. Howard proposed that there were not simply two alternatives—city and rural living—but a third possibility that melded them in a way that would offer the advantages of urban life as well as clean air, open space, and natural beauty. That would mean overcoming the boredom and lack of conveniences of rural living, at the same time correcting the overcrowding, unsanitary conditions, and morbidity of big-city life.

Among the attributes of a new rural-urban society would be nearness to recreation and the countryside, clean air, greater proximity of housing and job location to minimize transportation, recycling of refuse, nearby sources of food, and arrangements for the land to be owned as a unit, either publicly or in trust for the community, so that the increased real estate values created by the concentration of population could be credited to the people whose presence created these values. Such ideas have become increasingly relevant for both rich countries and poor.

Howard, in effect, had challenged the accidental city, and sought to achieve the economies of scale through an integrated urban region. He contended that a community should be able to achieve architectural and spatial harmony without making everything look the same; that urban people should not be insulated from their natural surroundings; that they ought to have outdoor sports and recreation nearby for their physical and mental well-being; and that these and other attributes of planned communities were not only socially desirable and physically sensible but could also be financially rewarding.

These ideas came to fruition after World War II in a score of British new towns, from Hemel Hempstead to Milton Keynes. The concept quickly spread to the Continent, to Asia, and to Latin America. Today, urban design to eliminate some of the transportation problems of the conventional city is a remedy made possible by improved regional transport and better communications. The trend toward designing the urban future is becoming more pronounced as the cost of accommodating congestion becomes prohibitive and as cities competing for new industries and jobs find it necessary to overcome the obstacles to moving in the metropolis.

Two European examples indicate the practical ways in which urban transportation and urban and regional design have combined forces to guide growth into more manageable communities, and how these programs affecting the suburbs have facilitated the redevelopment of older central cities.

In France, a decentralization strategy has been adopted which includes the building of new urban centers in the outlying areas of the capital region to disperse the growth of population and industry. In twenty years the center of Paris has lost 700,000 people, while the outer suburbs have gained 4 million. Mobility has made possible these shifts in population, and now a combination of transportation facilities and planned use of suburban land is helping to overcome the disorderly growth of the past.

There are five planned subcenters around the city's periphery (six to twenty-two miles out), connected by expressways and high-speed rails to the center. One-third of the new residents in the Paris area are living in these new cities, which are designed to guide suburbanization and to preserve open space. The Paris plan is also aimed at preparing the old city for renewal, and to reduce traffic volumes by achieving a better match of housing and jobs.

Providing the transport connections for new towns is the task of the regional express rail (RER) system, which operates over fifty-eight miles of lines and is designed to connect the two main railroad stations of Paris with its two major airports and the five new towns.

Part of the strategy of the Paris suburban developments is to overcome the exclusive concern for housing that characterized most suburban growth and instead to create a good mix of jobs and services, along with residential development. By providing a combination of housing, offices, government headquarters, recreation, and retail centers, it is hoped that much of the daily commutation and household travel will be localized. Without such an effort, the magnitude of the transport capacity required for commutation would mean not only tremendous costs but also unavoidable congestion. But for those who elect to live in the suburbs and work in Paris, the location and design of the outlying communities have made it possible to organize public transit along welldefined corridors leading to the center.

France has also taken steps to disperse urban development away from the Paris region. Cities in the provinces have been selected to become counterattractions to Paris; part of their attraction is that they are no longer isolated, due to air transport, motorways, high-speed trains, and telecommunications. Cities designated as equilibrium centers are given preference in the allocation of funds for public works, and this, together with other incentives and regulations, has helped curtail new construction in the Paris area.

In Sweden, roads and rapid transit made possible the development of planned suburban towns such as Farsta and Vallingby, and the transportation system has since been extended to include other major radial lines that serve a network of well-designed suburban centers. Station stops under or above ground provide access to the town centers of these communities. These centers contain a mixture of housing, shopping, and offices.

The organization of the Stockholm area around the radials of the expressway, railway, and rapid transit systems has been accompanied by measures to encourage public transportation. These include higher prices for downtown parking and traffic engineering that discourages driving to work downtown, such as one-way traffic, dead-end streets, and the conversion of streets to pedestrian and exclusive transit ways. The result has increased reliance on public transit for trips to the city's center. Densities in the central city have been reduced by providing good living environments in the suburbs; this has made possible the redevelopment of the historic center city. Although the Stockholm strategy failed to include suburban employment to the degree that might have been possible, other features of the system provide a useful model for the more rapidly growing urban areas of the world.

Growth Strategies in Asia

An ambitious strategy to reduce congestion through planned dispersal has been adopted in Japan, where the seemingly endless spread of urbanization in the Tokyo-Yokohama corridor has created a capital region of 25 million people living within a thirty-mile radius of the center of Tokyo. Fully 40 percent of all the nation's freight volume moves within this region or in and out of it, and the pickup and delivery of freight accounts for 30 percent of the street traffic in this city of two million motor vehicles. Commuters must spend long hours twice daily on critically overcrowded trains.

The nation's efforts to provide transportation for Tokyo and the populous corridor from Tokyo to Kobe have not only intensified urban crowding but have also drained resources needed to improve other urban services as well as the nation's backward rural regions.[9] The remedy proposed is a national network of new communities to be supported by telecommunications, air services, high-speed rail lines, expressways, and harbors. Transportation is recognized as "the most important strategic method" for the country's proposed regional redevelopment. Major long-distance travel facilities have already been constructed, and the high-speed "bullet trains" that operate from Tokyo are being extended. When the Japanese adopted the new comprehensive national development program they also passed the National New Trunk Line Build-up Law, to assure a network of high-speed surface travel to facilitate the nationwide dispersal of economic activities.[10]

Among the first of Japan's urban dispersal efforts is Tama New Town, west of Tokyo. It is a joint project of the Tokyo Metropolitan Development Corporation and the Japan Housing Corporation. Tama is eight miles long and one to two miles wide, and it includes development already present in four cities that are contained within the area. There are twenty-three neighborhoods in Tama, each having about 15,000 people, with their own schools, clinics, nurseries, social center, and convenience shopping. Although the New Residential Town Development Law prohibits industry in Tama, there are employment opportunities in offices and commercial establishments, and there will be jobs for three out of five workers within the city or nearby. Two out of five residents will commute to Tokyo.

Tama's main center contains the suburban railway station, department stores, restaurants, offices, banks, and a library. Smaller neighborhood centers are pedestrian areas (one modeled after Columbia, Maryland) protected from motor vehicle traffic and served by a network of walkways, which provide access to surrounding apartments.

A more recent project outside Tokyo is Tsukuba New Town, an academic city for national universities and research organizations, thirty-five miles from Tokyo Station. This planned center of learning is designed for a population of 120,000. Much of the new population has moved out from Tokyo as universities in the central city have left to make way for redevelopment. An automated bus system on guideways has been designed to unify the physically dispersed science city. The entire project is on about seventy thousand acres, but the planned city itself will cover only about 15 percent of the area, roughly equivalent to the size of many British new towns. Japan's magnetic levitation train is being tested at this location as a means of fast travel to Tokyo.[11]

Osaka has also completed two major satellites, each containing 200,000 people. Senboku New Town, which is on one side of Osaka, has extensive pedestrian and bicycle paths bordered by park land, giving the city ready access to recreation. A large number of private dwellings and townhouses have been built to satisfy the growing preference for low-rise housing and for automobile transportation. The prefectural government is in charge of the new towns outside Osaka, but the planning work is done by a team of planning and architectural consultants from both the public and private sectors. The other completed new town is Senri, which is nine miles from the center of Osaka and near the Osaka International Airport. About 85 percent of the workers in this town commute to the city by electric railway, which is an extension of the Osaka subway and was paid for as part of the new town. The fast ride has made this dormitory suburb attractive to white-collar employees.

The trend toward city-building in Japanese suburbs continues. Much larger preplanned cities are being designed for the Kobe area, where land is more plentiful. In the long run, the relatively undeveloped coast of the Sea of Japan will be the focus of new city developments to shift the population from the heavily congested area between Tokyo and Osaka. High-speed rail transport and communication networks will be relied on to make the new locations accessible.

Elsewhere in Asia, the congested conditions in Hong Kong have increased efforts to accommodate growth outside the built-up area. One example is the new community of Sha Tin, only a few miles outside

Kowloon (the location of Hong Kong's airport), but separated from it by high hills. Until 1970 the area was entirely rural. The city is designed to house 500,000 people. Several planned industrial districts have been developed, and the nearby campus of the University of Hong Kong encourages research firms, as well as government bureaus and professional services, to locate in the area. Total investment is divided equally between the public and private sectors.

Sha Tin is being built by the New Territories Development Department, established in Hong Kong's Department of Public Works, and operated by a team of town planners, engineers, and architects. Both public housing and private residential developments are included, along with industry and jobs, to assure a partially self-contained community less dependent on commuting.

Another Hong Kong project, Tuen Mun, on three thousand acres, is being constructed in forty-nine separate development "packages" with individual financing. Each includes carefully timed development of all elements that compose a workable community, including housing, schools, markets, open spaces, community centers, and recreation facilities.[12] The multicentered region and the new rail rapid-transit system form a combination that promises to increase mobility and access while improving housing and environment.

In the Republic of Korea, Seoul now has a population of more than 8 million, 20 percent of all the people in the country. One reason for the growth of Seoul is the superior services offered by the capital, which has most of the nation's universities, 40 percent of its medical facilities, and a major share of its cultural and entertainment facilities. It also has plentiful jobs, because much of the available foreign investment is centered in Seoul.[13] There are also growing disadvantages to living in rural areas where services are lacking and jobs are few.

Efforts to provide better urban housing and services in Seoul include the building of three new cities within the capital area to reduce the concentration of activity at the center. The new towns contain many large apartment buildings and provide sites for government offices removed from the old city. Two of these new cities are on the opposite side of the Han River from the center—an effort to encourage growth in that direction where densities are low.

Development strategy outside the metropolitan area includes major planned industrial cities accessible to Seoul by a national toll road system, which has sharply reduced the time and cost of transportation. One industrial complex is Changwon, which the national government has designed as a major production center. A variety of financial incentives are provided to attract foreign investors, including tax exemptions and loans to pay for land purchase, factory construction, and part of factory operating costs. The Changwon Industrial Complex Development Corporation has been the management unit in charge of creating this "industrial capital city."

Planned urban development has played a significant role in solving the transportation problems of Singapore. The highest priority has been assigned to housing, jobs, and amenities in planned suburbs; traffic congestion has been reduced in part through urban design.

From the air, the outlines of the multicentered regional city are clearly visible. Beyond the densely built-up old city are eight satellites surrounded by green space and interconnected by expressways. They provide modern apartments for half of the island's population of over 2 million. Yet twenty-five years ago the conventional remedy for the acute traffic congestion in the city's center would have been to expand the transportation system. An elevated railway was thought to be the logical answer, since the projected automobile numbers could not possibly be handled in a downtown area that had the same population density (85,000 persons per square mile) as Manhattan.

But Singapore committed itself instead to a massive housing program for low-income residents, opting against a heavy commitment for transportation. It decided to disperse population into suburban communities to make land available for better housing and neighborhoods and to reduce the concentration of activity in the central city. The suburban towns provided local jobs and relocated schools that once generated more downtown traffic than commuting workers.

Spending for housing at this stage of Singapore's development not only reduced traffic congestion in the old city but also saved enough money to build an additional fifty thousand three-bedroom apartments. At the average occupancy rate of 6 people per apartment, 300,000 people were moved out of the congested areas and accommodated in modern apartments for the price of an elevated railway. The decision to favor housing over transit, however, called for additional methods of untangling traffic. Ten private bus lines were consolidated into three regional companies, the public bus line was reorganized, over one hundred different routes and services were coordinated, and motorists were discouraged from driving downtown by charges for the privilege.

A motorist entering downtown Singapore in morning commuter hours must display a sticker, which can be purchased for U.S. $30 a month. Cars carrying four or more passengers pass without charge. One alternative is to drive to fringe parking areas and take a shuttle bus with a guaranteed seat. The other, which is more popular, is to ride the bus all the way. This so-called "congestion pricing" policy reduced morning traffic by one-fourth. The next step on the transportation agenda was

Figure Thirteen / A planned suburb in Singapore. Singapore Housing and Development Board photo.

the approval of an underground rapid-transit system made feasible by the quadrupling of Singapore's per capita income in real terms during three decades of reconstruction.

As the new cities and housing estates have become occupied by former slum dwellers and squatters, the exodus from downtown Singapore has made redevelopment possible. The government constructed new roads and pedestrian walkways in the city, provided parks and green spaces, and upgraded sewer systems and other utilities. Sites were sold to private developers for the construction of specified projects, including hotels, office buildings, department stores, garages, and apartments.

Singapore's regional development strategy has demonstrated the wisdom of resolving urban transportation problems in the broad context of the urban system as a whole. Transportation made possible the new suburban towns, as well as the redesign of the old city. Other Asian countries, unlike Singapore, are faced with the pressures of rural to urban migration and thus have far greater growth problems. But they also have some important advantages. Generally far more land is available around the big cities for preplanned suburbs, and there is not the same need to conserve space by resorting to high-rise apartments, which are both costly and rarely liked by their occupants. Usually there are intermediate-size cities, which can be improved to become attractive alternatives to the metropolis. Modern transportation and communication, as well as new sources of energy and new ways of providing sanitation, can be expected to increase the attraction of more dispersed urban communities.

Strategies for Latin America

In Latin America, a heavy concentration of population and economic activity in a few very large metropolitan cities has created massive traffic jams that detract from living conditions and increase production costs in the industrial sector. In the past thirty years, Brazil's urban population has doubled and the proportion of the people living in cities has increased from one-third in 1940 to about two-thirds in the 1980s. Brazil's 75 million urban residents are heavily concentrated in a few big cities, principally Rio de Janeiro and São Paulo, where traffic congestion is destroying many of the earlier advantages of living in these metropolitan centers.

Worsening traffic conditions have led to a major effort to bring the resources of the federal government to bear on the problem. The National Commission on Metropolitan Regions and Urban Policy was established to administer a federal aid program to assist the development of smaller metropolitan areas such as Curitiba and Pôrto Alegre, to promote development in remote northern cities such as Belem and Manaus, to help overcome the lack of development in Recife and other northeastern cities, and to further the economic growth of the capital, Brasília.

Air transportation was the key to making possible the construction of an entire new inland capital in the course of a single decade. The federal district that contains the new city is five hundred miles inland and is connected with Rio and São Paulo by an "air bridge" of nonstop shuttle flights. The city itself was designed specifically for movement by automobile, and its multilane expressways provide for uninterrupted travel most of the time. But with population and car ownership rising, the need for better public transportation is obvious, and walking in this auto-dominated city is virtually impossible because of the great distances between buildings and the hazards of crossing the street.

This metropolitan area of 1 million people has eight satellite cities twenty to thirty-five miles out, where twice as many people are living in such communities as Ceilandia, Taguatinga, and Braslandia. These unplanned areas of owner-built or government-supplied houses lining the dusty streets depend for their existence on employment in the federal city. But the trip is long, and public transportation service is either poor, entirely lacking, or too costly.

The solution for Brasília, as for other cities of the world, is to locate jobs accessible to housing or to provide housing where there are jobs. Transportation is part of the solution, but there is also the need to create employment opportunities within a reasonable distance of where people live.

Lucio Costa, the designer of Brasília, pointed out to me in an interview in Rio de Janeiro that the planned city was not designed to deny access and mobility to the poor who helped build it, as evidenced in the original plan: "The growth of slums, whether on the city outskirts or in the surrounding countryside, should at all costs be prevented. The Development Company should, within the scope of the proposed outline plan, make provision for decent and economical accommodation for the entire population."[14] Lucio Costa's ideas have been applied in the city of Curitiba, nine hundred miles south of Brasília. Curitiba has successfully used transportation to guide its growth and to improve the environment of the old city. In this metropolitan area of 1 million people, the transportation strategy has been to supply low-cost express bus service in the median lanes of major highways radiating from the business district, and to reduce downtown use of the automobile by a combination of high hourly parking charges and the creation of a pedestrian town center. Curitiba has also created a new industrial city on its outskirts to make way for rapid growth, and it has redeveloped the old city to provide good housing and services in pleasant neighborhoods.

Curitiba's planned industrial city covers six thousand acres of countryside, extending in a linear pattern at about six miles from the center. It is not simply an industrial park, the visitor is told, but industry in a park. Half the land is set aside for factories and about one-fourth for housing and open space. Thousands of workers are employed in the production of furniture, food and beverages, farm equipment, paper products, trucks, buses, and electronic equipment. They can either live close to their jobs in the new city or make use of express bus service from the central city. A public corporation, URBS, is responsible for both the transportation facilities and the new city.

The success of Curitiba's rehabilitation has accelerated migration from rural areas at a rate that threatens to inundate the city and to destroy many of the benefits that redevelopment has conferred. The response has been to design a program for dispersing development in the surrounding state of Paraná, with the focus on improving the condition of intermediate cities and upgrading living conditions and job opportunities in rural areas. The possibilities of this wider dispersal of urban

Figure Fourteen / An exclusive busway in Curitiba, Brazil. City of Curitiba photo.

activities will depend to a large extent on the ability to provide high-quality transportation and good communications as an inducement for industries to locate outside the metropolitan area. It is a challenge that many rapidly urbanizing nations will have to face.

But many interests are opposed to dispersal, as indicated by an aborted dispersal plan for the development of Bogotá, Colombia. This effort, which combined the talents of American, British, and Colombian city builders, ran into financial and political problems, and the planned cities designed to accommodate urban growth in the capital region were unable to attract the necessary support. The project is notable, however, for its breadth of concept and because the idea could be modified and salvaged as a prototype of the solutions that big metropolitan areas may eventually have to come to.

Bogotá anticipates a population of 9 million by 1990. Because the city is at an elevation of eight thousand feet on a relatively small plateau, surrounded by the Andes, the uncontrolled growth on the surrounding level land of the savanna would deprive the city of its nearby sources of food and destroy valuable recreation lands that need to be kept accessible.

The proposed solution to this problem began with a United Nations–World Bank study to help determine how future development might overcome the congestion of the old city, reduce the volume of commuting for low-income workers, make way for further growth, and do so in a way that would preserve the city's unique environment and prevent uncontrolled expansion into surrounding farmlands. The essence of the recommended development plan was to build three "new cities in the city" to accommodate growth, and then to restructure the central city to maintain a mix of living and working, and to preserve the cultural and institutional facilities located in the historic center. Approximately one hundred thousand jobs that do not need to be downtown would be siphoned off from the central business district into the new suburban towns. Offices and industries in the preplanned cities would be located within easy access of housing, thus reducing the volume of commuting to the center city.

The site selected for the first new satellite, Ciudad El Salitre, located on five thousand acres between downtown and the airport, was designed with help from the builders of Columbia, Maryland. It was expected to accommodate 500,000 people and to provide a minimum employment base of 125,000 jobs in manufacturing, business, government, and service activities. The El Salitre plan included a full range of social services, commercial facilities, open space and recreation, and a land-use pattern that would eliminate the need for an automobile. The entire development was to be self-supporting, partly by the capture of increased land values through rentals, sales, user fees, and taxes.[15]

A second redevelopment project in the old city would involve the opposite problem of introducing job opportunities and services in a residential area. Ciudad Kennedy, devoted exclusively to housing, has imposed substantial commuter problems on its residents who must travel long distances to find work. In this U.S.-assisted project it is hard to find any place to shop or to work—a good example of a mistaken transfer of American experience where it would do more harm than good. Techo, a new town-in-town, was designed to correct these conditions by supplying jobs to match housing.

Bogotá offered the hope that designing an orderly growth process and achieving an appropriate mix of land uses could substitute for more transportation and more congestion. Transport investments would be focused on road and transit connections to the planned new cities, and the growth being experienced in the Colombian capital could be absorbed without destroying the attractiveness of the inner city. Reviving (and revising) the plans for Bogotá might still make possible the orginal objective of managing growth through a partnership of transportation and planned urbanization.[16]

Planned dispersal is an equally urgent need for São Paulo, Brazil. Although a tremendous backlog of utility services has yet to be overcome, enormous new investments in transportation are scheduled to provide access to the central city for workers living in suburban *favelas*. But the cost of railway modernization to accommodate commuters and the staggering cost of São Paulo's rapid-transit system far exceed the city's financial capacity and threaten to deny many other needs, notably housing and the extension of health services and education.

São Paulo traffic in the rush hour seems the most frantic in the world until one witnesses the situation confronting Rio de Janeiro. Additional millions of people, expanding car ownership, and further concentration of jobs are causing bottlenecks of giant proportions and causing deterioration of the central city. Meanwhile the expansion of *favelas* on the urban fringes is creating untenable conditions of living. Massive unemployment prevails among low-income families. Jobholders encounter extremely difficult commuting problems. Rail facilities are inadequate and overcrowded to the point that serious injuries are regularly suffered by passengers in the morning and evening rush hours. Paying the railroad fare into the city is a heavy burden for people with limited earnings, and any relief through modernizing and increasing the capacity of rail facilities would entail prohibitive costs.

The task is how best to meet needs for housing, jobs, and basic services for the estimated 1 million Rio inhabitants now living in self-built shacks lacking in all basic services and amenities. Their relocation to government housing miles outside the city often intensifies their problems, for at peripheral locations it is difficult, if not impossible, to get a job. To go by private bus to Rio involves too high a fare, and it is not possible to avoid paying, as it often is on the railway. In a partial community without job opportunities, it is also impossible to pay even the subsidized government rents, and people resort to taking down doors and other removable objects to sell as a means of survival.

The example of Brasília's isolated satellites is a reminder that many of the lowest-income families cannot afford either housing or transportation. To help them, "sites and services" projects are providing land to persons unable to pay for ordinary shelter, to enable them to build a home in stages as cash becomes available.

But often the sites selected are on the city's fringes, where land is cheap but where there are no jobs, and transportation is either nonexistent or too costly. The need, therefore, is to include jobs as well as housing, and the attempt to do so is illustrated by the "metroville" program for urban development in Karachi, Pakistan. Karachi is expected to continue growing to the point where 12 to 15 million people could be living there by the end of the century, creating serious problems of water supply, sewage facilities, housing, and public health. Mass transportation facilities are heavily overloaded, and the possibilities of spending the sums necessary to modernize transport services are remote.

The urban growth plan proposed by a U.N.-sponsored study for Karachi accordingly recommended combining self-help housing with nearby jobs. A series of compact communities, with 40,000 to 50,000 people located within the metropolitan areas, was proposed as the most effective approach. People would be able to build their own housing within walking distance of schools, clinics, markets, and plants for light industry. Government interagency teams under the Karachi Development Authority were created to plan and develop the metroville sites. The first was situated close to an important source of employment—the Sind Industrial Trading Estate. Nine neighborhoods were created, each on about thirty acres. Metroville families were given the security of land ownership and jobs that could be reached without paying transport costs.

The metroville land-use plan allocated one-fourth of the area to the street system. The streets are used as extensions of the house, for social gatherings, recreation, and meetings. A main pedestrian shopping street is within easy access for all residents. The government supplies help for home builders through technical assistance in house construction and by selling building materials at reasonable prices.

The Karachi development program has exploited two major potentials for accommodating the world's rising urban population. One is the capture of the rising values of land created by community growth through rental charges, using the revenues to help pay public-service costs. The other is job locations that overcome the lack of transportation. Urban growth normally separates the lowest-income families from job opportunities and requires long trips from home to work. In the metroville, jobs are available in the nearby industrial estate. Space in the home is made available to enable workers to engage in making furniture, footwear, textiles, and jewelry and in operating shops. Thus the journey to work is eliminated.[17]

The Challenge for America's Cities

In the United States the persistence of heavy traffic volumes and nearly unmanageable commuter problems is focusing attention on the potential of mixed-use communities. This potential has been magnified by improvements in telecommunications which permit greater dispersal of economic activity and housing, but that call for the clustering of complementary land uses in order to keep development costs within bounds. The private sector has been the principal means of undertaking integrated city-building projects, with governments supplying public services in partnership with private builders.

Several privately created towns in the United States have demonstrated the possibility, including Reston, Virginia, and Columbia, Maryland, both built new as total communities designed to substitute for the conventional suburban housing development. Both models contain remarkably good ideas that could be replicated in other communities to improve the livability of America's surburban developments. The new towns have many advantages, both economic and social. Increased values captured by a single development corporation helped to pay for Reston's open space and amenities. Zoning regulations in effect at the time Reston was conceived would have meant dividing the land into uniform quarter-acre lots for 75,000 people, but the town accommodated the same number of people while preserving half the land in open space. Instead of building the project piece by piece, the whole community was designed in advance to create an internally consistent system of recreation, services, and jobs in a pleasant environment.

But these experiments (and other publicly aided new towns that followed) had a built-in disadvantage. They were inaccessible. Reston, for example, was built initially without public-sector help, and it lacked the necessary transport connections to Washington, which is twenty-six miles away. A private developer with limited resources for land acquisition was compelled to seek a fairly remote location where enough land could be purchased at a reasonable price. Lack of access meant that Reston was slow to develop, and job opportunities, which might have eliminated commuting for a larger part of the population, were slow to materialize. In the long run, however, Reston has proved to be well-situated, as nearby Dulles International Airport continues to attract more development along the travel corridor from Washington. In addition, Reston is now served by a toll road that greatly decreases travel time to the nation's capital. A successful pre-planned community must either be close in, built on a scale that permits substantial self-sufficiency, or provided with high-performance transport connections to an established city.

The same can be said of Columbia, Maryland. A private developer, without government assistance in the aquisition of land, found it necessary to locate where real estate was cheap but remote from Baltimore and Washington. Transportation from home to work involved excessive distances and generally required a second car because of the absence of public transportation. The advantages of managed growth would have been magnified by a national urban policy that provided assistance for land acquisition, infrastructure, and high-speed ground transport to complement the private-sector effort.

A federal program for planned urbanization was initiated by the Housing and Urban Development Act of 1970. It encouraged "well-planned, diversified, economically sound new communities," which could provide an economically viable alternative to disorderly growth, enhance the environment, and contribute to good living conditions. The program left unanswered such questions as where the new communities should be located, or how jobs were to be provided. There was no assurance that the new communities would be located close to big cities, or would be adequately served by transportation. Actually, the same limitations that plagued most private city-building efforts doomed the public effort. Federally aided new communities were located where a developer happened to own land or could acquire it at an affordable cost, and no effort was made to integrate community development with federally financed transportation. The program ended in bankruptcy.

Transportation and communications could be the key to a successful combination of inner-city redevelopment and preplanned surburbs. City-building efforts in depressed urban areas would need to include a comprehensive program of transportation and transit system management; the use of road funds to redesign, relocate, convert, and landscape streets and highways; the design and redevelopment of central city neighborhoods by private corporations in partnership with government;

and the provision of jobs and training for local residents. Simultaneous planned city-building efforts could guide suburban growth to avoid the mistakes that are duplicating inner-city problems in the suburbs.

Concentrating on transportation has too often diverted attention from other community needs and denied the interrelations between the transportation system and the total urban system. Redevelopment and predesigned dispersal could make use of transportation as an integral part of building more satisfying urban communities that combine livability with ease of access and mobility. Doing so would also remove major bottlenecks constricting the flow of traffic on national and international routes.

The hope that planned urbanization might someday provide lasting solutions for transportation problems through redevelopment and guided growth was put to rest, at least temporarily, in Hartford, Connecticut. Plans for the redesign and rebuilding of Hartford were made with help from the designers of Columbia, Maryland. The idea was to rehabilitate an area affecting 40 percent of the population and 75 percent of all the commercial and office properties in the city. It was decided to view Hartford and its twenty-nine surrounding communities as a single interrelated region, combining redevelopment in the old city with the construction of a new suburban community at Coventry, twenty miles out. The latter would substitute planned suburbanization for the planless spread of housing tracts and commercial blight. It would be part of the dual strategy of growth management and urban renewal. The Hartford plan experienced an early demise, but the ideas it contained might still be applied in another setting—Phoenix, perhaps, or Baltimore.

The redevelopment program aimed at creating cohesive neighborhoods of about 10,000 people, and supplying them with vocational training, day-care centers, shops, clinics, community meeting places, transportation, and recreation. The physical and economic models of the Hartford program indicated that the public investments programed to achieve these superior facilities and services would provide enough revenues through rents and taxes to cover the cost of all public investments over a twenty-year period. The results would make neighborhoods partially self-contained and transport-conserving. The program would be made possible by training people and giving them jobs in rebuilding the city itself, and by redesigning public services that were obsolete, in the wrong place, or aimed at the wrong objectives.[18]

Hartford planned an urban-growth strategy that originated in new towns. Only as much land as was needed for urban development should be so used, and the rest would be undisturbed countryside, farmland, and recreation areas. Normal growth trends in the Hartford metropolitan area were expected to use 30 percent more land than called for by the plan. The result would have been more crowding, while the development strategy proposed would preserve large areas of open space.

Creating a cost-effective growth pattern required the creation of an agency that would be responsible for physical, economic, and social planning, and a subsidiary corporation to handle the public and private financing and the actual development work. The new organization, the Greater Hartford Process, and its development corporation, DEVCO, were designed to make use of existing government agencies but to integrate their operations in a combined attack that would overcome the fragmented approach typical of conventional urban management. Yet Hartford could not muster political support, and the plan to build the new town of Coventry to accommodate part of the city's growth and overspill was resisted by local residents and had to be abandoned. The planners' dreams of rebuilding a city and preserving its surroundings were shattered.

Transportation helped build today's often crowded and disarranged cities, but now it can help to disperse them and to redesign and rebuild them. A large-scale effort at urban rehabilitation could provide useful jobs, train workers, stimulate construction, and make the cities more accessible. The billions of dollars spent for transportation could be pooled with other urban outlays in a long-term commitment to help make cities livable. In the United States, and many other countries, the need is critical. As René Dubos has stated, "if it is true, as it appears to be, that our environment and way of life profoundly affect our attitudes and those of following generations, nothing could be more distressing for our immediate and distant future than the decadence and ugliness of our great urban areas."[19]

Departure from the unplanned conventional city has become increasingly urgent with the growth of the global economy and the competition among cities for new industries and expanded markets. Competitive advantage lies partly in achieving efficiencies and low-cost output and partly in upgrading the local environment. The cost of production is influenced in no small measure by ease of movement within the urban area and by the availability of intercity and international transport connections. Attracting new investment in manufacturing plants and office headquarters is dependent on these factors as well as on the quality of the living and working environment.

Third World cities are especially in need of effective urban growth policies as their populations continue to multiply and as transportation costs become an increasing drain on scarce resources. It is probable that further rural to urban migration will eventually render the overburdened metropolis so unmanageable that a reverse migration will occur, following events already underway in developed countries. Population and economic activities will be forced into suburban and exurban areas. If this is to be the turn of events, then enormous advantage could be gained by anticipating the shift and preparing to handle it in an orderly way.

The situation suggests acquiring land around the big cities and beginning the construction of preplanned suburban communities now, to intercept part of the in-migration from rural areas as well as to accommodate outward movement from the central city. Doing so could avoid some of the heavy costs of growth in the older parts of the city while guiding development into a new urban environment designed for modern industry and served by road and air transport services suited to changing methods of manufacture. Legal provisions that permit rising land values to be captured to help finance suburban infrastructure could make a major contribution to economically viable new communities.

In affluent countries there is also a growing vulnerability to the high costs of conducting economic activities where transportation arteries have become clogged and the scarcity of land makes corrective measures impractical. The competition for new investment and for enterprising people will be won by communities that combine planned suburban growth with well-designed redevelopment of older areas, both aimed at greater ease of access as well as good housing and amenities. Accidental cities where the public sector is forced to spend inordinate amounts of tax funds to keep the traffic moving will be less able to upgrade other aspects of urban life that make cities fuller participants in the global economic network.

Five / Personal Mobility and Opportunity

The freight system has been a principal concern in formulating transport policies and programs for economic development, and passenger travel problems have been viewed mainly in the context of the journey to work. In much of the world, however, the amount spent for systems of travel now exceeds what is spent for goods traffic, and in economically advanced countries there is more travel for social and recreational purposes than for commuting. Altogether, the opportunities and extended horizons made possible by personal mobility play an important part in the American economy, while for many low-income countries the lack of such mobility has meant isolation and stagnation.

The changing picture can be attributed to the automobile and the airplane in particular, but to buses and trains as well. They have emancipated human beings from the immobility that once compelled most people to live and work in the immediate vicinity of their birth. Whereas in earlier times only soldiers, explorers, and the wealthy were privileged to travel any distance from home, the twentieth century has democratized mobility and has conferred its benefits on millions of ordinary citizens.

The most important aspect of the transport revolution is that for the first time the speed and range of movement have made possible a globe-girdling system that connects all of the continents with readily available transportation. The 200 million travelers that fly the world's international airlines every year have created a very different world than the one that the Wright brothers took off from earlier in the century.

The relation between travel and economic progress is reflected in comparisons between the per capita GNP of countries and the mobility of their citizens. Using an index number of one hundred to express per capita annual travel volumes in France, it was noted earlier that most economically advanced countries have a travel index of fifty or above. In the poorest countries, with only a few hundred dollars of GNP per capita, passenger mobility indexes are often no higher than two or three.

The relationships are understandable. Personal mobility is an essential ingredient of most economic activity, providing workers with a wide choice of jobs and enabling business to recruit workers from a large geographic area. Ease of travel has made it possible to transport large numbers of children to school and has added to the informal learning process that stems from contact with new places, people, and ideas. The airplane and automobile have multiplied the territory covered by sales and service workers and have enabled management to operate on a national and international scale. Plants can be located where conditions are favorable to production and marketing, but where there is also ready access for administrative and technical personnel from headquarter staffs. Ability to travel on the scale permitted by the automotive era and the age of flight has also created new consumer industries that are playing a dominant economic role, including tourism and recreation.

Mobility and Education

The delivery of education, knowledge, and information by way of schools and through the mails has been the traditional function of transportation, and history reveals the special advantages that resulted from the development of all-weather roads and the operations of rural school-bus systems. While rural transportation is justified principally on the grounds that it facilitates the movement of materials and crops, large benefits also accrue from the educational advantages made possible by ease of travel.

In an earlier period of American history, lack of mobility made it necessary to provide instruction within walking distance of widely dispersed farmhouses in numerous one-room schools. It was not an effective method of teaching, and only the motor vehicle and all-weather roads made it possible to change the system. After 1920, school buses transported students from a wider area to fewer but larger and better-equiped consolidated schools. The one-room schoolhouse, with a single teacher for as many as eight grades, began to disappear at the rate of four thousand per year in the twenties and thirties. By 1940, the move was on to create large regional high schools drawing students from a wide area served by bus. (In 1940, the United States had eighteen hundred high schools with fewer than 25 students and several hundred with fewer than 10 students.) Consolidated schools, well-staffed and well-attended, have now become one of the major educational contributions of a motorized America. Of the 61 million students enrolled in U.S. schools, colleges, and kindergarten or nursery schools, 34 percent still walk to school, but 16 percent arrive by car, and 44 percent ride in buses.

There are 745 million schoolchildren in the world, and getting to class is a universal problem. In Third World countries, a village that is not on an all-weather road may have no school or only a few, poorly staffed grades. Where there is a hard-surfaced road to the nearest town, the educational outlook changes. Teachers are willing to work in the village because it is possible to commute by bicycle or bus, and the school can expand to cover a large number of grades and additional subject matter. Children of the small villages who can be transported to schools in the nearest town not only benefit from greater educational opportunities but also find that contact with neighboring communities is itself a source of learning.

Improved education through transportation is having a major impact on health by helping people to understand the value of nutrition, the importance of safe drinking water, and other methods of health care. Schooling for women, which is furthered by the availability of bus transportation, is of special importance. Women are responsible for about half the work connected with agriculture and food processing, and they (as well as men) prove to be more productive in farm work if they have had a primary education and have participated in village literacy programs. Studies in several Latin American countries also have shown that women who have completed a primary school education are able to upgrade child care and nutrition and have an average of two children fewer than those who are uneducated. It has been concluded from World Bank data that only about one-third of the economic growth rates around the world can be attributed to capital formation and that much of the balance is due to improvement in the capabilities of human beings.

The transportation of knowledge and information is now being supplemented by telecommunications to extend the content and geographic coverage of instruction, while jet travel has made much of the world accessible to travelers whose knowledge was once derived almost exclusively from books.

Teilhard de Chardin has summed up the educational role that transport is playing in the stepped-up evolution of knowledge. There are two principal factors at work, he says: the roundness of the earth and the speed and range of modern transport. Human beings on the limited surface of a sphere have come into closer association because of their increasing numbers and their ability to travel, which have made possible personal contacts and the exchange of ideas on an ever-widening scale. Transport, now supplemented by communications, has permitted work and thought to be shared with colleagues all over the globe, stimulating new ideas, promoting joint undertakings, and fostering an increased rate of mental achievement throughout the world.[1]

Travel and Development

Humanity has just begun to benefit from the revolution in personal transport. Throughout most of history people have suffered a travel disadvantage compared to other forms of life. Fish and whales are frequent travelers, noted for their endurance and navigating capabilities, and some land-based animals such as the antelope and cheetah can cruise at speeds close to the fifty-five mile legal limit on American highways. A chimney swift, on a normal day, may fly five hundred to six hundred miles in elapsed times that exceed the best efforts of the motorist, while a golden plover can fly nonstop between the U.S. mainland and Hawaii without restrictions on departure dates, routing, stopovers, or length of stay.

Human beings, however, not being endowed with either the speed or the range enjoyed by fish or fowl, have spent much time and money inventing ways to circumvent their limitations. Impressive technological victories have been won, as today's mobility attests. As recently as 1872, Jules Verne could only imagine going around the world in eighty days, and the record set some years later by the clipper ship *Nellie Bly* was still as much as seventy-two days. It was not until 1924 that the airplane was able to cut the round-the-world record for sailing ships in half. Now, on a U.S. or Soviet space shuttle, time around the world is no longer eighty days, but ninety minutes.

The total number of international travelers landing at U.S. airports, including citizens of all countries, now exceeds 20 million a year. There are thirty-one thousand travel agencies in the world, with combined earnings of a quarter of a trillion dollars a year, and hotels and motels supply eight million rooms in 130 countries to house the visitors.[2]

Tourism is such a new phenomenon that the meaning of the word escaped most people until the mid-thirties, when efforts to provide paid vacations for workers began to bear fruit. At first it was believed that such diversions from work would be a blow to productivity, but eventually the effect was found to be positive. On a global basis, in 1980, some 500 million workers were entitled to have time off for holidays with pay, half of them in Europe, 30 percent in the Americas, and the rest in Asia and the Pacific. Longer vacations are increasingly common as technology has increased output per worker and has reduced time on the job.

World tourism receipts now exceed the value of all the iron, steel, ores, and metals that move in international trade. Nations with 20 million or more visitors a year include Spain (39 million), Canada (33 million), France (29 million), Yugoslovia (22 million), and the United States (20 million).

Wide-bodied jets provide speed and comfort far superior to the air services available only two decades ago. Fares have declined by a substantial margin compared to the thirty-one cents a mile from New York to London thirty years ago. Various package tours have made travel cheaper and easier for the uninitiated, and intensive efforts are being made in most countries to provide the necessary backup—hotels, roads, trains, buses, familiar diet, potable water, and cultural attractions. The number of hotel rooms in the world is expected to double by the start of the twenty-first century. They will be needed if tourism, as it now appears, becomes the world's largest industry by the year 2000. Meanwhile the age-old hazards of travel—including inclement weather, fire, collisions, and piracy—have been augmented by ship and airline hijackings and by terrorist acts. The gravity of current threats to security confronts the world with a major challenge if the benefits of growing international passenger traffic are to be realized. In addition, the ability of people to change countries with relative ease of travel, as illustrated by the movement of foreign workers across national boundaries, has led many countries to use restrictive measures on both economic and social grounds. The trends are not unlike protectionist measures to limit imports of manufactured goods.

The intercontinental transport system, mainly by air, has resulted in an extensive relocation of the world's people, with major implications for future world development. The capacity for long-distance travel has contributed to the vast numbers of immigrants, refugees, displaced persons, and migrant workers. In the United States there is wide-spread evidence of the new Asian presence, with numerous recent arrivals from the Republic of Korea, Vietnam, and other Southeast Asian countries. In addition, people of Spanish origin now living in the United States number close to 15 million.[3]

Nearly 14 million migrants had temporary jobs in Western Europe in the seventies, traveling periodically from Turkey, Yugoslavia, Morocco, and many other countries. In the Middle East, there are several million more workers who have traveled from their homelands of India, Pakistan, Burkina Faso, Nigeria, and Egypt.[4]

These migratory movements made possible by modern mobility have had bad effects as well as good; the former include family disruption, the drain of skilled workers from developing nations, and the creation of friction between local people and visitors from basically different backgrounds and cultures.

On the positive side, new arrivals from other cultures are adding to the skills and services available to their host communities, and are contributing to the output of local economies by helping to compensate for the shortage of workers. From the standpoint of developing countries, major exporters of labor to Western Europe (Algeria, Greece, Morocco, Tunisia, Turkey, and Yugoslavia) are the beneficiaries of billions of dollars of remittances from migrant workers to their families. The total realized in a single year is equivalent to one-fourth the value of all exports from these countries. And the Middle East has benefited

Table Ten / Trends in Travel Time

Year	Method	Elapsed Time in Days
I. *Around the World*		
1872	Jules Verne—Imagination	80
1889	Sailing ship—*Nellie Bly*	72
1924	U.S. Army Aircraft	35
1929	*Graf Zeppelin* Dirigible	20
1947	Pan American Airways Constellation	4
1981	Space Shuttle *Columbia*	0.06
II. *Across the Atlantic (New York–London)*		
1905	Sailing Ship—*Atlantic*	12
1938	Steamship—*Queen Mary*	4
1981	Aircraft—*Concorde*	0.15

Source: Newspaper Enterprise Association, *The World Almanac and Book of Facts* (New York, 1986), pp. 147, 151–53.

Table Eleven / Foreign Visitors per Year, Selected Countries

Country	Millions of Visitors	Country	Millions of Visitors
France	33.6	Portugal	3.7
Spain	25.6	Ireland	2.3
Italy	22.1	Thailand	2.1
United States	20.4	Japan	1.6
Austria	14.4	Egypt	1.5
Canada	12.9	Brazil	1.4
United Kingdom	12.5	Argentina	1.3
Federal Republic of Germany	11.3	India	1.3
		Turkey	1.2
Switzerland	9.2	Israel	1.1
Belgium	6.6	Malaysia	1.0
Yugoslavia	5.9	Australia	0.9
Greece	4.8	Kenya	0.4

Source: United Nations, *Statistical Yearbook, 1983–84* (New York, 1986), pp. 985–87.

from the millions of constructions workers from abroad who have helped build the modern infrastructure needed to further the development goals of oil-exporting countries.

Although many nations maintain regulations and tighten quotas to limit the flow of people across their borders, the trend is toward a further dissolution of international barriers to travel as air transportation increases the ability to move great distances quickly and cheaply and as global communications help to ease the way for the many who elect to change countries. Nations that bar the intercontinental movement of people and ideas may find that restrictions on global travel can cause whole societies to fall behind in an age when cross-cultural innovation and discovery have become major contributors to economic progress.

Travel in the Industrial Countries

Growth of the travel network in the United States is measured by the fact that in 1900 the mobility of the average person was only 436 miles per year, almost all of it travel to work.[5] There was neither time nor income for pleasure trips. Since 1900, the rapid growth of car ownership and, more recently, the rising volume of air travel have increased per capita annual travel in the United States to twelve thousand miles. Not all this travel is essential to economic growth, as indicated by the fact that people in high-income European countries do less traveling—perhaps six thousand to eight thousand miles per capita a year. But all nations with high per capita incomes depend on relatively high levels of domestic travel to support their economic and social progress.[6]

Over half a billion U.S. intercity trips each year extend for one hundred miles or more from home. Automobiles (including trucks carrying camping equipment) account for four out of five of these journeys, and airplanes account for most others. About half the trips involve a round-trip distance of two hundred to four hundred miles, but one-fifth are for journeys of one thousand miles or more. The primary purpose is to visit friends and relations (one-third of the total), while business and conventions generate one out of five trips and recreation accounts for almost as much. Social and recreational travel is predominant on the airlines (58 percent), as well as on the railroads (63 percent).[7]

Railroads, buses, cars, and the airlines share in providing intercity travel. In many developed countries the railroads play a key role in supplying high-density movements over intermediate to long distances. Japan is the leader in such services, generating twenty times more rail passenger travel than the United States. Per capita rail travel is about twelve hundred miles a year in Japan, compared to thirty miles in the United States. The Soviet Union is the second country most dependent on rail travel, accounting for sixteen times as many passenger-miles a year as the United States.

Japan's high-speed, electrically powered rail system has cut in half the elapsed time on the 310-mile run between Tokyo and Osaka. The

Table Twelve / Domestic Intercity Public Transportation Trends, United States

Year	Passengers (in millions)			
	Air	Bus	Rail	Total
1940	3.0	140.9	452.9	596.8
1945	7.1	481.9	891.1	1,380.1
1950	18.9	338.5	486.2	843.6
1955	41.3	237.8	432.0	711.1
1960	56.8	366.0	325.9	748.7
1965	92.7	378.0	298.7	769.4
1970	155.0	401.0	283.9	839.9
1975	191.1	351.0	269.4	811.5
1980	275.2	365.0	300.2	940.4
1984	323.6	362.0	310.6	996.2
1985	360.6	358.0	301.2	1,019.8

Source: Transportation Policy Associates, Transportation in America (Washington, D.C., March 1986), p. 9, and, for 1985, Transportation in America, Update (Washington, D.C., July 1986).

Shinkansen (new trunk route) was built on an entirely new right-of-way to avoid the congestion of the old route, with its mix of fast and slow traffic, its more than one hundred stations, and its thousand grade crossings. Operated by computer from Tokyo, the sixteen-car blue and cream Hikari and Kodama of the Japanese National Railways provide departures every twenty minutes for a fast and safe journey, which passes through sixty-six tunnels along the mountainous route. In their first two decades of operation, the 120-mile-per-hour trains accommodated over 2 billion passengers, but high operating and maintenance costs, and competition from cars and airplanes, have left the system deep in the red. The Japanese Diet has enacted legislation calling for construction of some four thousand miles of new high-speed train routes in a national network aimed at achieving greater dispersal of population and economic activity. But the future of high-speed transport may now lie in getting off the ground (magnetic levitation), to avoid track wear and to increase safe speeds. Meanwhile the decision was made to reduce huge Japanese National Railways losses by dividing the system into six companies during 1987, gradually privatizing the network through the sale of stock, closing unprofitable lines, and eliminating redundant employment.

Conventional rail systems have been undergoing extensive modernization, however, in Europe, where the speed of the passenger train makes it possible to travel to distant cities for meetings and to return the same day. The Trans-European (TEE) trains provide 100-mile-per-hour connections among major cities, and Très Grand Vitesse (TGV) trains in

France are competitive with airline services, reaching speeds of 180 miles per hour on their exclusive rights-of-way. British Rail provides fast and frequent schedules for travel between London and most United Kingdom cities, affording a high degree of comfort and reliability.

In the United States domestic airlines account for seven times as many passenger-miles of travel as the railway and intercity buses combined. After deregulation, the air fare on many main lines was cheaper than bus transport, which had always been the low-cost method of passenger transport. Continuing progress in aircraft design and performance promises to increase the air share of domestic intercity travel, including many parts of the developing world, where the time and expense of surface transport are often excessive, and where geography and topography make many destinations relatively inaccessible except by air.

The automobile, however, is by far the most important means of personal travel in the economically advanced countries, not only for short-distance movements but for long-distance ones as well. In both Europe and North America, most trips over one hundred miles are made in the family car because of its economy and convenience and because long-distance travel has been facilitated by the expanding network of motorways, which permits uninterrupted movement at sustained high speeds. While the 42,000-mile Interstate Highway System and other expressways in the United States exceed the motorway networks of any other country, many nations are well-equipped with roads of comparable design. Italy and the Federal Republic of Germany each has over three thousand miles of motorways, and other countries with over six hundred miles include The Netherlands, Belgium, France, Great Britain, Spain, South Africa, Mexico, Japan, and the Republic of Korea.[8]

The proportion of total annual passenger-miles of travel by car is 85 percent in Canada and the United States, 80 percent in France, 75 percent in Australia, the United Kingdom, and Italy, and 50 percent in Japan.[9] Sixteen industrial countries have at least one passenger car for every five people, and many middle-income nations have entered the motor age in recent years. Countries with over one million cars include Argentina, Brazil, Venezuela, Mexico, the Soviet Union, Poland, Yugoslavia, the Democratic Republic of Germany, and Czechoslovakia.

Adding the various travels of the average American, the total expenditures for mobility have increased from less than 6 percent of a small household budget in 1900 to over 14 percent of the many times larger amount of family income available in 1980. Consumers now spend $500 million a day for mobility, and only food and housing command a greater allocation of consumption expenditures than travel.

Among the many impacts of passenger travel has been the creation of

Table Thirteen / Trends in Consumer Expenditures for Transportation, United States

Year	Total[b]	Private Transport	Local Public Transport	Intercity Public Transport	Proportion of Consumer Expenditure for Transport
		Billions of Current Dollars			Percentage
1909	$ 1.5	$ 0.7[a]	$0.5	$ 0.3	6.2
1929	8.0	5.8	1.1	0.6	9.9
1949	20.2	16.1	2.1	1.1	12.1
1981	260.8	240.5	6.8	13.5	14.1
1985	349.8	320.3	7.2	22.4	13.5
		Percentage Distribution			
1909	100	44.3	33.3	18.1	
1929	100	72.5	14.1	7.0	
1949	100	79.5	10.3	5.3	
1981	100	92.2	2.6	5.2	
1985	100	91.5	2.1	6.4	

[a] Mostly horse and carriage.
[b] Includes foreign travel; therefore total exceeds sum of items, except in 1909, when foreign travel was less than $0.1 billion.

Source: Twentieth Century Fund, "Transportation," in America's Needs and Resources (New York, 1955), pp. 272, 274; U.S. Department of Commerce, Survey of Current Business (Washington, D.C., July 1977 and July 1986), pp. 29 and 38, respectively; and Statistical Abstract of the United States, 1982–83 (Washington, D.C., 1982), p. 605.

a new industrial sector devoted to recreation, sports, and leisure activities. In the United States, an average of 123 days a year are available for nonwork activities, and weekends and holidays make it possible for large numbers of people to take off by car. Lodging industry revenues per year are close to the $20 billion mark, and the roadside motels of big chains such as Holiday Inn, Sheraton, Hilton, and Ramada have become symbols of the nomadic tendencies of the motoring public. The automobile plays the major role in outdoor recreation, most of which requires driving to the scene. Regular passengers include some 94 million golfers, tennis players, skiers, hunters, and fishermen. Millions of acres in government parks such as Yellowstone and Grand Canyon are accessible for sightseeing, touring, and camping. Visitors to national parks have increased from 1 million in 1920 to 332 million in 1984, and in the air age millions come from abroad.

At what point can it be expected that travel demand will taper off? The answer involves a combination of time, money, and technology.

The amount of time available for travel is obviously limited by other demands on a 24-hour day. Of the 168 hours in the week, Americans sleep 55 hours and work 32 hours. Of the remaining 81 hours, nearly half (38 hours) is available for leisure and relaxation. The amount of time that can be devoted to travel is likely to increase with a further shortening of work hours. A congressional study has estimated that travel time will increase from the equivalent of thirteen full days a year in 1975 to twenty days in the year 2000. Projected urban transport would consume two-thirds more time in 2000 than in 1975, partly due to congestion, and the intercity travel time was projected to increase by more than a third.[10]

If average cost per mile were to remain constant, and consumers, as at present, spent an average of 14 percent of disposable income on travel, a doubling of disposable income by the year 2000 would mean that twice as much mobility could be afforded. Declining average costs would permit more travel, assuming that more travel hours were available. But choice of technology will influence the result. Travel by air makes it possible to generate more mileage in a given period of time, but it is also more expensive per hour. Two people making a trip by car may spend $10 and cover fifty miles per hour. But two people traveling by air may spend $100 and cover five hundred miles per hour. Money budgets, rather than time budgets, then become the key restraint, and, if the proportion of household budgets for transport remains at 14 percent of total expenditures, consumers who wish to travel more will have to do some reshuffling of their trip patterns. More long-distance and international trips might be possible by spending less for local and routine transportation, relying more on telecommunications for some journeys or on collective means of getting to work in urban areas.

Travel in Developing Countries

The volume and radius of travel in rich and poor countries reveal enormous gaps. Travel per capita in low-income countries averages between three hundred and four hundred miles a year—about a mile a day.[11] In most developed countries the figure is at least twenty times greater. These data indicate that development in low-income countries will depend, among other things, on placing a higher priority on the movement of people. The question is how best to accomplish desirable gains in personal mobility and what transportation strategies will be required to cope with the limited horizons imposed by the absence of travel opportunities.

Personal mobility in developing countries is achieved to a large degree by methods not recorded in transport statistics: walking, bicycle riding, and the use of animals, animal-drawn carts, and country boats.

Table Fourteen/Visitors to U.S. National Parks and Monuments

Year	Number of Visitors
1904	121,000
1920	1,058,000
1940	16,755,000
1970	172,000,000
1984	332,000,000

Source: Bureau of the Census, *Historical Statistics, Colonial Times to 1970* (Washington, D.C., 1915), and *Statistical Abstract of the United States, 1983–84* (Washington, D.C., 1986), p. 224.

Table Fifteen/Annual Hours of Travel per Capita, United States

Type of Travel	Hours per Capita	
	1975	2000
Local		
Urban	186	299
Rural	39	48
Total local	225	347
Intercity		
Air	1.9	4.5
Auto	95.3	127.9
Bus	2.3	2.1
Rail	.5	.4
Total intercity	100.0	134.9
Total travel hours (local and intercity)	325	482

Source: National Transportation Policy Study Commission, *National Transportation Policies* (Washington, D.C., June 1979), p. 231.

The transportation scene in the developing world suggests that much of the population is on the move at any given time, and a large volume of passenger traffic occurs because people are the principal carriers of freight. Along the roadways everything from wood and water to hay and bricks is headloaded, carried on the back, or suspended from poles. This kind of travel, while essential to economic activity and to supplying the household, is not recorded as part of the formal transport system. If it could be, it would be more aptly classified as the movement of freight rather than of people. Even travel by bus and rail includes substantial numbers of passengers whose travel purpose is to carry chickens, vegetables, and the products of cottage industries to urban markets.

Travel properly classified as personal mobility consists mainly of the trip to work by bus and train, or longer distance intercity travels by rail and highway, much of it for social and recreational purposes. These trips account for the estimated six hundred miles of annual per capita passenger movement in low-income countries, and the fifteen hundred to two thousand miles of travel per person in middle-income countries.

Passenger transportation in Indonesia illustrates the importance of travel by road. The fifth largest nation, Indonesia has 150 million people and a per capita income of $750. Over 90 percent of all travel is by highways, with railways accounting for only 4 percent of the total, and air and water travel for another 4, equally divided. Travel by road in 1980 was made possible by 4 million motorized vehicles, including 2.6 million motorcycles. They accounted for twice as many passenger-miles as the nation's 700,000 cars. Travel data do not include nonmotorized transport performed by the pedal-driven *becak* (bicycle rickshaw), which has such an important presence on the streets of Jakarta. About 40 percent of all motorized traffic is generated in the cities, and, judging from the auto-clogged multilane boulevards of Jakarta, a high percentage of Indonesian urban traffic is concentrated in this capital city.[12]

In Bangladesh, one of the world's poorest countries (with per capita income of $140 per year), a different pattern emerges. This low-lying and densely populated country of 90 million people is so vulnerable to flooding in the monsoon season that many roads and bridges are under water, and only high embankments reduce the washouts on main road and rail lines. Water and rail transport accounts for about half of the movement of passenger traffic, and the other half is by road. Ninety percent of all rail operations are passenger trains, which are so jammed that frequently there is no space left on the roof. But most travel in this predominantly rural country is by bullock carts, bicycle rickshaws, and country boats. Road conditions are often extremely poor, and there is only a mile of road per 1,000 inhabitants (compared to a mile for every 100 people in France).

The more affluent Philippines (with per capita income of $560 in 1983) has already reached the stage when the rising curve of automobile ownership has passed well beyond the upward curve of motorcycle ownership. Yet most Filipinos are too poor to own a car, and they have come to rely on a highly satisfactory low-cost substitute, namely the group-riding jeeps known as jeepneys. There are 85,000 of these vehicles in the Philippines, and, while there is always at least one jeepney in sight throughout Manila, it is also a principal means of travel between cities. Jeepneys generate more passenger-miles of travel in rural areas than in urban ones, and altogether their operations throughout the country exceed automobile travel by 50 percent. When one adds the travels per-

Figure Fifteen / A crowded bus. World Bank photo.

formed by the nation's 125,000 vans (compared to only 18,000 buses), it is apparent that collective transport services provided by small vehicles on frequent schedules offer a good substitute for both the automobile and the bus. Other developing countries have their own successful versions of what are often called group-riding taxis or public automobiles, providing affordable motor transportation for low-income people.

For higher-income families and middle-income countries, the private automobile is preferred over publicly provided passenger service, and the upward trends in car ownership continue. There are ten million cars in Asia (excluding Japan), eighteen million in South America, and seven million in Africa. The total of thirty-five million units has been climbing, and it would be much higher were it not for restrictions on car ownership imposed by many countries on grounds that the car is a luxury or that the importing of vehicles and petroleum constitutes an unacceptable drain on foreign exchange. Although some developing countries (Argentina, Brazil, Mexico) have one car for every 8 to 15 people others (India, China) have only one car for every 700 to 10,000 people.

A frequently expressed view is that motorization should be minimized in favor of concentrating on more basic requirements—food, clothing, shelter, education, and various services such as water and sewage disposal. It is believed that if low-income countries limited their consumption to what is important for development, the automobile would not be very high on the list of what is needed.[13] Yet there is an apparent connection between the motorized society and the affluent society, for the latter owes much to the incentives, jobs, opportunities, and productive activities that stem from automobility.

In Europe, automobiles were long viewed unsympathetically by governments. Cars and fuel were heavily taxed; little was done to build or improve highways and parking facilities; and both rail and transit facilities were heavily subsidized to help them compete with the automobile. These negative policies were the opposite of the approach to the automobile in the United States, where taxes were kept low, highway programs were subsidized, and transit and rail facilities were neglected. The results have not been very different. Europeans adjusted by making smaller and more economical cars, by suffering higher accident rates and greater traffic jams, and by parking on sidewalks. They did not, however, give up the idea of driving.

In the mid-fifties, the Japanese viewed the possibilities of motorization in their country with alarm, fearing that lack of metals and petroleum would invite serious balance of payments difficulties. They also believed that the resources required to create a road network would stifle postwar recovery. Yet the decision thirty years ago to triple the road budget and to build a national system of expressways financed with the help of tolls (and the World Bank) helped to make Japan the world's largest producer, and the second largest owner, of motor vehicles. For the Japanese, motorization has been a major factor in promoting exports and in accelerating the growth of high-tech industries.

Up to a certain point, however, there is no ncessary connection between automobiles and economic progress. Nations can be moderately prosperous without motor vehicles, and relatively poor in spite of them. But a point is reached when being without automobiles generally means being without good roads. Truck transport alone cannot justify road construction of the magnitude required to serve developing economies. After a certain level of per capita income has been reached (generally about $2,000 in 1981 dollars), the automobile becomes an important ingredient of economic growth.

The upward trend in motor vehicle ownership appears to be irreversible, and the question is how to achieve the most advantage from the car

Figure Sixteen / A crowded train. World Bank photo by Tomas Sennett.

while reducing its unwanted side effects. The important step is to avoid the excessive traffic afflicting big cities rather than to forego the automobile altogether. Personal mobility and the extended radius of activity made possible by the car can be boons to development. In low-income countries the movement of technicians, teachers, doctors, agricultural extension workers, and other specialists has been greatly facilitated by access to rural areas by car and jeep. Automobiles that pay for their use of the road system also help finance facilities needed for freight.

For most families in low-income countries, the possibility of owning an automobile is precluded and other methods of increasing personal mobility will have to be relied upon. Further progress in road-building offers the opportunity to make greater use of bicycles, with the prospect of eventually upgrading one's transportation to motor scooters or motorcycles. While millions of two-wheelers are now operating in Asia, and bicycles are often the dominant vehicle in urban rush-hour traffic, a shift from bicycle to motorized two-wheelers will be repeating the experience of European countries after World War II. At that time the scooter played a major role in personal transportation, and sales of two-wheelers far exceeded those of new cars. But in the early fifties car sales began to outnumber scooter and motorcycle sales in the Federal Republic of Germany, France, and other West European countries. The same trends can be anticipated in a number of developing countries.

A second possibility for increased personal mobility is the shared use of the automobile. As noted earlier, this is already a major means of mobility in the cities of developing countries. The jeepney of the Philippines, the *por puesto* of Venezuela, and the *dolmus* of Turkey have popularized the concept of the "public automobile." An extension of this service to rural communities through cooperatives or other farm organizations might provide a measure of mobility for village people who are now either completely lacking transportation links with the rest of the country, or who must rely on buses that provide uncertain, irregular, and inconvenient services for most local rural travel.

A third possibility for increasing passenger transport capabilities in rural areas may be in the expanding number of trucks and tractors owned by farmers in more prosperous countries. The small pickup truck is ideal for carrying out a combination of freight-carrying chores and family transportation. (Fourteen million of the forty million trucks in the United States are declared by their owners to be used principally for personal transportation.)

It may also be possible for the automobile industries of Japan, Europe, and the United States to market a minicar that is rugged and has a sufficiently low price to be an attractive purchase for farm families. Although vehicles of this kind have been marketed in the past with a generally negative response, recent alliances among the world's major auto manufacturers and the growing numbers of potential car buyers in developing countries may create a more favorable climate for the minicar. Joint ventures aimed at satisfying this kind of need might be a first step toward creating new markets. Included would be rural businesses and farm operators seeking the benefits of greater personal mobility for themselves and their families.

A major difference in the economic impacts of the motor age is reflected in the degree to which domestic industries contribute to automotive production and employment. Where vehicle imports are the source of motorization, many of the economic benefits of the automobile are not realized. Cars that use many of the same parts made in different countries increase the possibility of locating vehicle manufacturing and parts production in developing countries and increase the prospects that these countries can benefit more fully from the motor age.

There is evidence that personal mobility is critical to the achievement of economic and social progress. Separate indexes of mobility for freight and passenger transport indicate that there is often a closer relation between per capita income and travel than there is between income and freight movement. Most countries with an exceptionally high index of per capita income also have a high travel index, while their freight

Table Sixteen / Passenger Cars in Selected Countries, 1983

Selected Countries	Millions of Cars	People per Car
United States	126.7	1.8
Canada	10.9	2.3
Australia	6.5	2.4
France	20.9	2.6
Federal Republic of Germany	22.6	2.7
Sweden	3.0	2.8
United Kingdom	16.6	3.4
Japan	26.4	4.5
Spain	8.7	4.4
Ireland	0.7	4.9
Israel	0.6	7
Argentina	3.5	8
Singapore	1.1	9
Brazil	10.5	12
Mexico	4.9	15
U.S.S.R.	10.3	26
Colombia	0.5	56
Egypt	0.6	76
Indonesia	0.9	191
India	1.0	740
China	0.1	10,220

Source: Motor Vehicle Manufacturers Association, *Facts and Figures '85* (Detroit, 1985), pp. 34–35.

indexes are often low. Conversely, countries that have a high rate of freight mobility are not always high in income, and this lower rate of economic achievement is often accompanied by a low level of personal mobility. (See table three, p. 10.)

This suggests that the developing world will need to place greater emphasis on overcoming obstacles to the movement of people. Part of the answer lies in placing a higher priority on public transportation in cities and on intercity routes. It may also be possible, for both city and intercity travel, to further adapt the private automobile to public use. While the group-riding taxi or jitney taxi has become the special means of personal mobility for the poor, it has always been opposed by the better organized public carriers in the cities. The key role played by taxi operations calls for preferential treatment for such vehicles in the use of street space rather than restrictions on their operations.

Table Seventeen / Trends in World Automobile Registrations

Year	World Total (Millions)	Population per Car	Percentage in U.S.
1940	37.2	59	74
1960	98.3	29	63
1965	139.8	23	54
1970	193.5	18	48
1975	260.2	15	41
1980	320.5	14	38
1984	364.8	13	35

Source: Motor Vehicle Manufacturers Association, *Facts and Figures '78* (Detroit, 1978), p. 31; *Facts and Figures '86* (Detroit, 1986), p. 35.

The Role of Telecommunications

Many of the purposes that cause people to travel could be accomplished more quickly and less costly through the movement of information rather than people. Modern telecommunications spell good news for both the affluent countries that are coping with excessive travel volumes and the less developed countries that lack the basic means of personal mobility. For the latter there is now greater hope for some of the development impacts that would otherwise have to await the costly and protracted process of building extensive networks of transportation. For both rich and poor, the prospective evolution in methods of communication could prove to be a breakthrough of major consequence.

At one time transportation was the only way to communicate over any distance. Runners and riders in relays were the formal means of spreading the news. In the United States, it was the duty of landowners to deliver official documents across their properties to the nearest neighbor, who was expected to do likewise. Eventually, postal officials took a special interest in advancing transportation by designating post roads to be given priority attention and, later, by subsidizing the airlines through air-mail payments.

Telegraph and telephone services broke the link that had made transportation and communications one, and the gap was widened by radio and television. Now, with the speed, economy, and capacity of computerized information systems, fiber optics, and communication satellites, many communication functions performed by road, rail, and air can be accomplished through electronic transmission.

Thus far communications and transportation have grown at closely comparable rates. In 1980, the United States had 35 percent of the world's telephones and 37 percent of its motor vehicles. Europe had 37 percent of the telephones and 35 percent of the vehicles. In 1980 the average American made two and a half trips per day and three telephone calls. Among U.S. families, 99.9 percent had radios and television sets, and 82 percent owned automobiles. In the future, however, the paths of transport and communications can be expected to diverge as the use of communications media per capita outstrips travel per capita.

The probable impacts on transportation will affect all four subsystems—the intercontinental, urban, intercity, and rural networks—and the effects may be quite different. In some cases the net impact may be to promote travel, while in others the ability to communicate will supplement or substitute for transportation. For intercontinental transport, for example, the installation of trans-Atlantic and trans-Pacific fiber-optic cables will greatly expand business communications and personal contacts. But the enormous capacity of the voice and video services throughout the world will multiply interpersonal relations and, as a result, stimulate travels and meetings abroad. Tourism will also be encouraged by the increasing familiarity with other parts of the world and by the ability to use the communications net for making arrangements and for keeping the traveler in touch with home. How much travel growth can be anticipated will depend in part on airline fares and the speed and convenience of travel, but all signs point to further progress in these areas.

In urban areas, improved communications and computerized information systems, video-tex, videophones, and other innovations open the way to a greater dispersal of economic activity and employment. The need for concentrating offices in city centers is reduced, and the location of offices in suburbia and in the home or neighborhood will be encouraged. Telecommunications may not only lessen the number of persons commuting on crowded urban expressways but also, for the largest and most congested cities, there may be no other way of dealing with the difficulties of getting to work. The automated office may lessen the number of people needed to operate information-based activities, reducing the number of working hours or days and helping to spread the commuter traffic over longer periods.

The effect of communications on intercity business travel may be substantial as firms take advantage of the economy of communicating rather than traveling. Many business meetings can be conducted effectively by teleconferences, at much lower costs in time and money. Large meetings and conferences held in less desirable cities or at inconvenient times will also be susceptible to the substitution of telecommunications. In essence, it will be possible to choose between travels that are satisfying and those that are routine, monotonous, and unwanted. Thus, the volume of intercity travel will be expanded by technological advances in transportation, but a reduction of unwanted trips will occur at the same time as telecommunications offer new ways of doing business.

In the less developed parts of the world, the expansion of telecommunications to previously isolated rural areas will permit the performance of services once dependent on travel. But contacts with the outside world via television and telephone will also lead to multiplying contacts with other parts of the country, and to greater pressures for building new transportation connections. The end result of establishing communications may be the extension of the transport revolution to areas previously bypassed. To the extent that economic development is promoted by the breakdown of isolation, rising incomes will permit more travel and more widespread ownership of automobiles. Countries in which annual per capita travels are now only 360 miles per capita (India, China) will be advancing toward the 1,500 miles per year typical of many middle-income developing countries (the Republic of Korea, Brazil).

For the world as a whole, therefore, developments in telecommunications can be expected to increase opportunities and choices rather than effect any net reduction in total travel volume. But there may be major changes in the types and purposes of both business and personal travel, and in trip length and geographic distribution. Travel volumes, total and per capita, can be expected to continue their rapid rise, creating boom conditions for the automobile industry and the airlines. The shift in emphasis from work trips to other travel purposes will continue, with higher rates of growth for long-distance, as compared to local, travel.

In summary, the global transportation network will be increasingly dominated by the movement of people rather than goods and materials. In developing countries, commuter traffic will increase with the growth of industry and the expanding work force. Equally pronounced will be the upward trend in travel associated with education and the desire for wider contacts and the discovery of new opportunities stimulated by television. Both rural and urban populations will place greater value on travel as a means of extending horizons.

In the already developed countries, where social and recreational travels and personal business trips already far exceed the volume of work trips, rising incomes and declining work hours will make it possible to take advantage of the increasing speed and convenience of transportation for long-distance and foreign travel. Several factors will cause

Table Eighteen / The Communications Gap, 1983, Selected Countries

	Telephones per 100 Persons	Television Sets per 100 Persons	Radios per 100 Persons
Developed Countries			
Sweden	89	38	38
United States	76	79	204
Switzerland	79	38	36
Canada	66	46	131
Denmark (1980)	64	36	38
New Zealand	61	29	89
Netherlands	58	45	79
Finland	57	36	99
Australia	54	42	130
United Kingdom	52	48	99
Federal Republic of Germany	57	36	38
France	54	38	86
Japan	52	58	71
Less Developed Countries			
Paraguay	2.3	2	8
Philippines	1.5	2	5
Egypt	1.2	3.3	14.3
Honduras	0.9	1.3	5
Malaysia	6.6	6	15
India	0.5	0.2	6
Pakistan	0.5	1	8
Ethiopia (1980)	0.3	0.1	0.8
Indonesia (1980)	0.3	0.9	4
Nigeria	0.2	0.6	7
Bangladesh	0.1	0.1	0.8

Source: Bureau of the Census, Statistical Abstract of the United States (Washington, D.C., 1986), p. 845.

per capita travel to increase more rapidly than per capita freight movement. There will be a decline in the relative importance of heavy industry, an increase in the importance of services, a reduction in the transport requirements of the energy sector, and a wider application of
transport-conserving processes in agriculture and industry. But factors
capable of effecting a reduction in per capita travel, including telecommunications and changing urban design patterns, will be more than
offset by economic and technological changes stimulating personal
mobility.

Six / Marshaling the Necessary Resources

Population trends and the growth of industry on a global scale will generate substantial increases in the volume of world transportation. The trends will require massive new outlays for construction and maintenance in both the rich countries and the poor if the transport sector is to be responsive to mounting needs. New technology and more relevant institutional arrangements will be necessary, along with strategies influencing transport demand as well as supply. The critical challenge will confront the developing countries, where the lack of capital and the dearth of technical and managerial skills continue to frustrate efforts to overcome the transportation deficiencies that stand in the way of all other efforts to accelerate development.

Without adequate transportation in the developing countries, neither the city nor the countryside can make its full contribution to world economic growth. The system will have to be extended. The costs, however, are forbidding, and they call for changes in domestic policies, as well as more effective international aid efforts. Questions addressed in this chapter are, first, how best to marshal the domestic resources of low-income countries, which will have to assume the main burden, and, second, how to increase international technical and financial help in ways that best supplement domestic programs.

The transport systems that serve the vital needs of both the rich and the poor countries are almost always in financial trouble. Obsolete equipment, deferred maintenance, operating deficits, and bankruptcy are common conditions worldwide, regardless of whether ownership and management are public or private. The world's railroads are typically in the red. Urban public transport rarely pays its way, and national subsidies are counted on to build highways, ports, and airports and to keep the transportation network operating.

Various reasons explain why this is so, from protecting infant industries to prolonging dying ones. A succession of new transport techniques has created damaging competition for established modes, prompting powerful interests to press for government assistance. Poor financial showings are also the result of pricing transportation services too low either because of the difficulty of determining the relevant costs in an industry with large overheads and joint uses or because of management's desire to retain certain types of traffic, even at a loss, rather than succumb to competing carriers.

An additional financial problem may result from the desire of governments to assist various industries, geographic areas, or classes of citizens by charging them less than what it costs to accommodate traffic. It may be political suicide to attempt to charge remunerative rates. Automobile interests are generally sufficiently powerful to obstruct any efforts to charge car owners the marginal costs of rush-hour use of the streets, and highway or trucking interests may object to tax increases needed to keep pace with inflation. The attempt to take economic reality into consideration has resulted in riots, revolutions, and the banishing of public officials. Bailouts have thus become the preferred global solution, and billions of tons of freight, as well as countless numbers of passengers, benefit from a continuing transportation windfall.

The financial problems of transportation also stem from the fact that many of the benefits of transportation are external to the system and should rightfully be paid for by nonusers—for example, land owners and developers. Another factor is the separate and independent administration of the publicly provided infrastructure and of the several transport modes. Losses in one part of the system need to be balanced by surplus revenue elsewhere, but this is precluded by failure to acknowledge the need to balance losses and gains to achieve a satisfactory overall solution. For example, feeder routes that do not support themselves through user charges contribute to the traffic flowing onto the main lines that generate surplus revenues.

Financial difficulties also result from economic regulations or other forms of government intervention. For many years, U.S. regulatory commissions usurped the functions of railway management and denied rate adjustments needed to provide the necessary revenues to pay for modernization. Regulation also denied the carriers permission to arrange for acquisitions that would create more effective intermodal systems. It was not until 1980 that regulatory reforms gave management greater flexibility in rate-making, permission to engage in other forms of transport, and leeway in abandoning noncompensatory routes and services. At the local level, for many years state public utility commissions denied passenger fare increases and prevented modernization. The results are still evident in the subway systems of older cities and in the general condition of public transport in the United States.

Applying American experience in the search for effective financial arrangements in developing countries, therefore, requires recognition of the many negative elements in the picture. European handling of urban public transit and of railway passenger service may be more relevant, whereas freight handling by Europe's railways is more likely to yield negative examples. Perhaps the most useful experience for today's developing countries lies in the efforts of the United States and other countries to institute user charges to help pay for highways, airways, and other public facilities.

User Charges for Transportation

In the early stages of development, when little traffic is being generated, the high initial costs of transport facilities cannot be borne by users. But experience demonstrates the financial wisdom of making a start, with the goal of working toward high levels of self-support. In the United States, where the gasoline tax was first introduced in 1919, the trend toward greater reliance on user taxes has continued. Recently, the condition of the federal budget has prompted renewed efforts to make the transport sector financially more self-sufficient. The experience provides some insights for other countries that have made only limited attempts to exact payments for use of transportation facilities and to credit them to a fund that is drawn upon to assure continued maintenance and expansion.

The federal government has been recovering from users about half the money being spent for all types of transportation annually. About 95 percent of federal outlays for highways are now being collected through a nationwide tax on motor fuel and through excise taxes on vehicles and related items. About 43 percent of airway expenditures and 5 percent of waterway outlays are being recovered. User charges are also levied by the fifty states and are an additional source of revenue for road-building. Altogether the motorist is paying about 70 percent of the total bill for streets and highways.[1]

The merits of levying appropriate fees and user taxes to defray the costs of public infrastructure seem clear. Having users foot the bill introduces economic considerations into investment decisions that contribute to the efficient use of resources. From the standpoint of the transport industries, the advantage of user taxes lies in the knowledge that a predictable and sustained source of funds will be available to maintain and extend the facilities, in contrast to the uncertainty of relying on periodic appropriations of general funds. And general tax funds are more urgently needed to support public functions for which a user charge is inappropriate, such as education, parks, and social services.

The United States has now embarked on the process of putting inland waterways on a user-charge basis, beginning with a tax of a few cents per gallon of fuel consumed, with increasing rates over time. Airways are also being paid for through an aviation trust fund that receives the revenues generated by an aviation fuel tax. These charges to defray the costs incurred by government will enter into the costs and charges paid by transport users.

It may now be necessary to explore more direct methods of payment for major highways in the United States, where the Interstate Highway System is subject to periodic shortfalls in the amounts available for maintenance and replacement, and changes in the rates are dependent on legislative action by Congress. The Interstate System is financed by a share of federal taxes levied on all motorists, regardless of whether they use the system. For developing nations, as well as for the United States, considerations of equity suggest that special licenses or tolls be collected from vehicles actually using the major highways. The collection of charges that cover costs may be the most effective method of assuring maintenance and replacement funds and of reducing unnecessary travel.

Tolls are a supplemental road financing method in the United States, and over two thousand miles of the Interstate Highway System are toll facilities. Some of them were among the nation's early demonstrations of modern road design. The initial demonstration was the Pennsylvania Turnpike, opened in 1940, and built on the right-of-way of an abandoned railroad. It was financed by a federal grant that covered 45 percent of the cost, plus a loan from the federal government's Reconstruction Finance Corporation. Tolls were charged to pay off the loan. The new road resulted in large savings in truck operating costs, made possible by nonstop driving, reduced travel time, increased safety, and the lower grades provided by the partially completed railway roadbeds and tunnels. Since that time toll financing of major highways has proved successful in a large number of states, including Maine, New Hampshire, New Jersey, New York, Pennsylvania, Ohio, Indiana, and Illinois.

The alternative of depending on periodic congressional legislation to increase federal user taxes means that political factors may prevent timely increases in rates to keep pace with needed maintenance and replacement. This was the case when the recent five-cent-per-gallon fuel tax increase was delayed far beyond the date when preventative maintenance was needed to avoid a damaging deterioration of the Interstate System. Even the passage of the new legislation (four cents for highways and one cent for transit) has provided no more than a holding action to prevent further deterioration. Still higher charges will be required to bring the system back to conditions of a decade ago, leaving unsatisfied the need for further improvements to meet growing traffic demand.

A national toll road authority responsible for a self-supporting Interstate System would provide the necessary flexibility in setting rates and would make it possible to charge vehicle users for the specific costs of their operation on the network. If those who actually drive on the system were charged, highway users as a whole would no longer be asked to subsidize those who travel on the interstates. It would also be possible to allocate more user tax revenues to other primary highways, which have suffered from a concentration of funds on the 42,000-mile Interstate System. For these roads the ratio of federal to state cost-sharing is 90–10, whereas for other roads the federal government matches state funds on only a 75–25 basis.

Japanese experience indicates how a combination of tolls and general taxes was able to help build a system of modern roads well in advance of the time that self-support could be counted on. In 1956, Japan's highway Route One between Kobe and Nagoya was a tortuous stretch of dusty gravel riddled with potholes. Truck drivers wore dust masks to combat the clouds of surface debris stirred up by passing vehicles. The Ministry of Construction, impressed by the new toll highways in the United States, was eager to adopt similar financial methods to begin the task of upgrading the national system to modern design standards. The trouble was that Japan had few motor vehicles that could help to pay the cost. Total registrations for the whole country numbered less than a million, most of them three-wheelers in local delivery service.

At the time, it was argued by many Japanese that a nation well-endowed with rail transport and coastal shipping had no need for roads, that low per capita income (U.S. $450) prevented private car ownership, and that the prospective number of motor vehicles could not possibly provide enough support to warrant toll financing. In any case, Japan had no petroleum, and imported fuel would cause critical balance-of-payment problems if road transport were to be encouraged on any large scale. These misgivings failed to take into account the developmental impacts that were to follow from a program that provided the country with good roads.

An American team invited by the Japanese government to survey the prospects for motor transport contended that although rail and water transport were doing an excellent job in moving raw materials and heavy bulk shipments, they were not able to provide the services demanded by the newly developing industries manufacturing high-value electronic equipment and machinery. Moving these items on the railway system was causing heavy losses in damaged goods, and the cost of protective packaging was a burden on industry. In addition, delays in transit were resulting in canceled orders and the loss of overseas customers. If motor transport were available to supply the factory and to provide fast delivery of finished goods, it would be possible to provide the kinds of service needed to help Japan compete in overseas markets. The foreign exchange earned as a result would more than pay for imports of petroleum and raw materials. And good roads might further the ownership of

Table Nineteen / Government Expenditures for Transportation, United States, 1985
(Millions of Dollars)

	Federal	State and Local	Total
Airways	2,290	—	2,290
Airports	879	3,700	4,579
Highways	14,452	39,882	54,334
Rivers and harbors	1,189	1,300	2,489
Rail (AMTRAK)	917	—	917
Urban transit (UMTA)	2,787	6,667	9,454
Total	22,514	51,549	74,063

Source: Transportation Policy Associates, "Transportation in America" (Washington, D.C., March 1986), p. 16.

Table Twenty / Road Transport Trends in Japan

Year	Motor Vehicles (Millions)	Truck Transport (Percentage of Ton-miles by All Methods)	Highway Expenditures (Millions of U.S. Dollars)	National Toll Roads (Miles)	National Toll Roads (Percentage of Total Highway Expenditures)
1950	0.3	8	62	—	—
1955	0.8	12	144	—	—
1960	1.8	15	555	—	14
1965	6.0	26	1,166	190	18
1970	15.5	39	3,111	649	19
1975	27.0	36	13,334	1,888	17
1980	36.4	41	25,221	2,860	16
1985	46.2	46	32,236	3,721	15

Sources: Road Bureau, Ministry of Construction and Japan Road Association, "Roads in Japan, 1985" (Tokyo, 1985); Japan Automobile Manufacturers Association, "The Motor Industry of Japan, 1986" (Tokyo, 1986); and Japan Highway Public Corporation, "1986 General Information" (Tokyo, 1986).

private cars and increase the scale of vehicle output, thus reducing costs per vehicle. Japan might even export motor vehicles!

The Kobe-Nagoya toll expressway had little chance of early self-liquidation, but long-term traffic projections suggested that self-support would eventually be possible. General taxes would have to be provided in the interim, but tolls could help to pay the bill from the start. On this basis, the 160-mile highway was built as a modern divided highway and financed with the help of a World Bank loan. Part of the financial strategy was to provide a much higher level of user support for all roads through an increase in the taxes levied on motor vehicles and fuel. The ratio of user charges to GNP was tripled from 0.6 percent to 2 percent.[2]

The first toll expressway quickly reached a position of self-support. The road was extended from Nagoya to Tokyo, and a national system of four thousand miles, to link all of Japan by modern expressways, is nearing completion. Motor vehicle registrations increased from 0.8 million in 1955 to 46 million in 1985, and in three decades Japan became the world's leading motor vehicle manufacturer, the leading exporter, and the second most motorized nation.

The procedures and rationale behind Japan's road development efforts suggest a useful strategy for developing countries. Foremost is the desirability of charging users some part of the cost of construction from the start. The combination of user taxes and tolls can begin the trend toward a self-financing system. This procedure has been followed by the Republic of Korea and, to a lesser extent, by other developing countries. India, China, and Brazil are among the logical candidates for toil financing and for dedicating fuel taxes to a special fund for roads.

The Situation in Third World Countries

The gap between financial needs and available revenues in the transport sector of Third World countries is widening at a damaging rate, and insufficient measures are being taken to halt the trends. Many of the world's most populous nations rely to a major degree on rail transport for both passenger and freight movement, and these publicly supplied services are often a legacy of colonial days, when domestic development was not the concern of transport planners. Changing conditions often find rail-oriented economies saddled with unprofitable routes that political pressures make it difficult to abandon. Such considerations may result in the railways hiring large numbers of unnecessary workers, and job security for civil servants frustrates efforts to trim labor costs. The resulting high costs and low productivity are not compensated by adjustments in rates and fares, since railway management is generally prevented from exercising managerial responsibilities. Political considerations make it extremely difficult to alter charges or tailor services to changing demand brought about by economic and demographic factors and by the growth of competing carriers.

The result is that national budgets are strained in the effort to cover railway operating deficits, whereas investments needed for replacing worn-out facilities and equipment are far behind schedule. Services thus continue to deteriorate and large volumes of traffic that might have been retained are lost, to motor carriers in particular. The problem is worsened by the foreign-exchange requirements for imported equipment and for the payment of debt service on past loans. Extensive bilateral and multilateral lending for rail facilities was based on overoptimistic traffic projections and was not accompanied by the policy revisions and upgraded performance necessary to assure the railways of their appropriate role in the total transport picture.

Meanwhile the increasing amounts of general tax revenues needed to keep the rail systems operating have become a burden on the tax payer and have meant less support for highways, which are carrying an ever higher percentage of the traffic. Road vehicles generally pay large amounts to national and state governments through special vehicle and fuel taxes and other levies, but the revenues from such imposts are not earmarked for highways, and what is spent by governments on road construction and maintenance is likely to be a small fraction of what is collected.

These deep-seated and politically sensitive problems have their roots in the evolutionary progress of transport technology and the understandable resistance to change on the part of established bureaucracies, vested commercial interests, and a wide variety of regional and local interests. Based on recent salutory trends in the United States, solutions appear possible in a combination of increasing user charges and economic deregulation, plus greater reliance on private operations as a means of depoliticizing the tasks of moving people and goods.

In those developing countries where a major part of intercity passenger and freight movement is by railway, the task of achieving a greater degree of self-support lies partly in a better knowledge of costs and the establishment of rates and fares based on appropriate cost determinations. People and goods are too frequently moving on the wrong subsystem due to a combination of inadequate cost accounting and inaccurate pricing. Computers promise to help overcome these problems and to further the realization of efficient intermodal systems that distribute the traffic burden on rational economic grounds. The current situation in most countries is the reverse. Each method of transportation attracts traffic on the basis of false signals resulting from charges that fail to reflect appropriate cost considerations.

To illustrate, in India the rates on certain bulk commodities are equalized for the country as a whole, with the result that industrial plants that base their location and market strategy on average transport costs can disregard the economic consequences of distance. The demand for freight movement is consequently higher than would otherwise be the case, and resources devoted to transport are being wasted. Many important industries also enjoy freight rates that are subsidized on the grounds that the aided industries are especially important to the economy. Although the Ministry of Industry makes up the difference in payments, the effect is to artificially stimulate traffic and worsen already congested conditions on the rail system.

Cities in developing countries confront two related problems in financing urban transportation. The streets are clogged with motor vehicle traffic that is not paying directly for the costs incurred, and this in turn is creating volumes of movement that congest the system and compel heavy investments in expressways and rapid transit. Charging motorists the cost of providing street capacity is a remedy that might reduce some unnecessary or marginal trips and could add substantially to the revenues available to the city. But in most countries the political power of automobile owners has thwarted attempts to impose charges that reflect more closely the outlays required to accommodate the traffic. The most hopeful remedy is the Singapore gateway experiment, described earlier, that demonstrates the advantages of congestion pricing to the city. This solution needs to be augmented by traffic engineering strategies that ban the private car from certain areas and that give preference to mass transport.

Rural transport confronts more difficult financial problems. Rural areas cannot increase road revenues by charging the users, because traffic is so light that costs per unit of traffic would be excessive. There is also no way to make better use of facilities through traffic engineering when the facilities are generally nonexistent. But a broader system view of the problem may help to resolve the dilemma. The character of local roads is changing, and the roads' financial requirements suggest the need to revise conventional views of the functions they perform. At one time local roads were built for strictly local use, and there was little national interest in these types of facilities. But local roads today are often local only in a geographic sense, for they serve as the origins and destinations of traffic in food, minerals, and forest products which is not only national but also international. Building and maintaining such roads are necessary for carrying out the broader tasks of feeding the world and supplying its factories.

International Financing Assistance

The poor condition of existing transport facilities and the new investment needed to keep pace with growth indicate that domestic measures will not be sufficient to cope with the financial woes of Third World transport. Many countries need far more foreign help if they are to realize the financial resources and the technical and managerial skills that will be required. The transportation systems of the developing countries have been helped substantially over the past three decades by financial support from individual nations and international agencies. During the first decade and a half of lending by the World Bank and its affiliates, much of the emphasis was on transport, which accounted for 35 percent of all loans. In Asia, Africa, and the Middle East transportation financing was well over 40 percent of the total. Nearly half the amounts made available went for railroads and one-third went for highways. Ports were also a significant part of the program, accounting for 13 percent of the total.

Since that time, the emphasis on transportation has declined as other aspects of development have gained recognition, especially education, health, and other elements of aid for developing human resources. The decline has brought transport lending to less than 15 percent of the World Bank's total operations. Total bank lending has so increased, however, that the absolute amounts available for transport during the last three years of the seventies were nearly twice as much as in the first seventeen years of World Bank transactions. Taking inflation into account, there has still been much greater support for transport in recent years. The Inter-American Development Bank has also allocated substantial funds to transportation and communications, despite a decline in the relative amounts made available for this sector, from 15 percent of the total over a twenty-year period to 10 percent in the past several years.[3]

Transportation projects, however, have still been insufficient in most bilateral and multilateral programs. In addition, the future amount of economic assistance may decline with lower growth rates in donor nations and the reduced flow of private capital resulting from debt repayment problems in recipient countries. By the mid-eighties a combination of unfavorable factors had caused total debt service payments of developing countries to exceed the amount of new economic assistance. More money was flowing from the poor countries to the rich than from the rich to the poor.

The types of transportation assistance provided by international lending agencies are illustrated by a few examples of World Bank projects undertaken in 1980. In Bangladesh urban bypass roads were built to facilitate traffic moving from the captial to the port of Chittagong. Brazil was loaned several hundred million dollars for rail rapid transit along a populous access route to Pôrto Alegre. Railway realignment was undertaken in the Congo to help develop its forest resources, and the construction of secondary and farm-to-market roads was made possible by loans to Ecuador, Nigeria, and Ghana. These projects included technical assistance in road maintenance and planning and in other institution building. Loans to the Philippines were used to help improve port operations, and major dock and harbor construction was undertaken in Tunisia, Tanzania, and Uruguay.

Project assistance is concentrated in a relatively few countries in any given year. During 1986, the transportation projects approved by the World Bank and its affiliated International Development Association (IDA) included twenty-two countries. Three of them (China, Indonesia, and the Republic of Korea) accounted for over half the $1.5 billion total.[4]

Official development assistance from the aid-giving countries and international agencies for all purposes amounted to approximately $37 billion a year in 1981–82.[5] Assuming that as much as 10 percent was made available for transportation, the transport allocation would total $2.5 billion annually, available to some one hundred countries. This is one-twentieth of the amount spent annually for basic transportation facilities in the United States alone.

The need for greater financial support for developing countries led the Independent Commission on International Development Issues to support the U.N. objective that donor nations should allocate 0.7 percent of their GNP to foreign assistance. In the commission's view, the allocation should be raised to 1 percent by the end of the century. The following table shows how far the present situation falls short of the goal. It was also recommended that a series of automatic revenue transfers be instituted through international levies on trade and travel, which would provide support for a World Development Fund to supplement existing lending institutions.[6]

In recent years, numerous suggestions have been made that attempt to incorporate automatic features into international financing by some type of world tax or assessment that would make possible a consistent and predictable source of aid. While the problem of automatic revenue collection involves the entire aid effort, the transport sector may be a practical place to start. For example, international traffic using sea and air routes that are provided free by nature might pay a nominal user charge to help finance domestic facilities in less developed countries. This would transfer some of nature's largesse on the intercontinental system to land transport, which lacks the built-in advantages that were conferred on sea and air transport.

A world tax collected on energy, travel, trade, or other transactions, and dedicated to a world transportation fund, might provide an acceptable way of extending the global transportation system. Part of the returns from the sale of petroleum have already been directed into development programs through the aid made available by Saudi Arabia, Kuwait, Venezuela, and other oil-producing states. Each one-cent tax on a gallon of internationally traded oil used for transportation would

Table Twenty-one / Cumulative World Bank and IDA Lending for Transportation
(to 30 June 1985)

	U.S. Dollars (Millions)	Percentage
Airlines and airports	$ 316	2
Highways	13,472	53
Pipelines	118	—
Ports and waterways	3,822	15
Railways	7,012	28
Transportation sector	656	3
Total transport	$ 25,396	100
All sectors	149,604	
Percentage of transport		18

Source: World Bank, *Annual Report, 1985* (Washington, D.C., 1985), pp. 164–65.

Table Twenty-two / Aid Donors of the World (1981–82 Average in Millions of Dollars)

	Official Development Assistance	Share of ODA	ODA as Percentage of GNP
United States	$ 7,040	18.8	0.24
European Economic Community	12,400	33.2	0.53
Japan	3,160	8.4	0.29
Canada	1,180	3.2	0.42
Sweden	950	2.5	0.91
Australia	770	2.1	0.49
Norway	520	1.4	0.92
Switzerland	240	0.6	0.25
Austria	340	0.9	0.51
Finland	140	0.4	0.29
New Zealand	70	0.2	0.29
Spain	240	0.7	0.13
Ireland	30	0.1	0.17
Luxembourg	10	0.0	0.17
OPEC countries	8,180	21.9	1.49
Centrally managed economies	2,140	5.7	0.13

Source: Organization for Economic Cooperation and Development, *World Economic Interdependence and the Evolving North-South Relationship* (Paris, 1983), p. 70.

produce a fund of $2 billion a year. According to a Brookings Institution study, "the means of mobilizing large financial resources for international purposes exist and can be made to work if the political will is present."[7]

Not all countries would be likely to agree to instituting international user charges, but a beginning could be made by major nations toward a continuing supply of funds to help the poorest countries. Revenues from an international transport levy could be credited to the IDA to help replenish the funds available for transport on a regular basis.

Another possibility might be an international levy on the factory sales of motor vehicles. With current production levels at forty million to fifty million vehicles a year and bound to go higher, a 1 percent levy could produce over $4 billion annually. The rationale for such a tax lies in the new markets that could be created for the automotive industries by accelerated road-building. Obviously the greatest further potential for vehicle ownership is in areas of the world which are immobile and most in need of motor transport.

The Brookings study of international financing acknowledged that governments were not yet ready to accept the idea of a world tax, but that the possibilities should be aired "as a means of helping concerned people in all parts of the world to think concretely about the steps that may have to be taken if growing international needs are to be met."[8] The continuing debates over foreign aid appropriations and IDA replenishments suggest that the time is approaching when a concept once considered politically utopian will prove economically compelling.

Conventional loans through the World Bank and other international agencies can be expected to continue as the principal means of financing specific major projects such as ports, airports, toll highways, and railway modernization. But the accumulating debt problems of many developing countries suggest the desirability of shifting the emphasis to grants for countries in special need, and particularly for the extensive construction and maintenance requirements of rural roads.

A useful model for international grant assistance is found in the federal-aid program for U.S. highways. The federal government initiated an aid program for rural America which began in 1916. The United States did not lend funds on a project basis, but made available a continuing program of grants for a system-wide attack, with funds distributed among the states on the basis of population, area, and road mileage.

Federal assistance was made contingent on the designation by each state of a federal-aid road system constituting 7 percent of total mileage. Grants had to be matched on a 50–50 basis, design standards had to be adhered to, and maintenance of aided roads had to be at acceptable levels if aid were to be continued. A later program for secondary routes tied the program to rural development objectives: routes serving school buses, mail delivery, and milk collection. Federal commitment to a continuing program made it possible for highway departments to plan their construction programs with the assurance that funding would be sustained, permitting them to carry out advance land acquisition, develop long-range plans, build effective institutions, and establish competent staffs.

Developing countries could enter into similar agreements with international financing agencies, based on appropriate stipulations as to matching requirements and design and maintenance standards. Selection of eligible roads would be based on the concurrent undertaking of rural development programs to be served by the transportation improvements. A road program would also need to be supplemented by assistance for installment financing of motor-vehicle purchases by farmers, farm cooperatives, or businesses. As indicated earlier, the use of trucks is predominantly connected with the operation of farms and industry, or with the delivery of services such as telephone, electricity, and water. Developing countries need vehicles as well as roads if transportation is to support development.

Grants could also be made available to help finance road-rail coordination. Countries that have extensive railway systems and that are prepared to convert to intermodal freight and passenger networks might be encouraged to do so through international grants and accompanying technical and managerial assistance. Such aid could help to establish the kinds of multimodal transport companies that have recently begun to emerge in the United States in the wake of deregulation and that have operated successfully in Canada over a period of years. Transportation system grants could be an important means of extricating Third World nations from the destructive conflicts between road and rail which have no legitimacy in efforts to further economic development.

The private sector could also be a greater source of international aid. In 1980, private loans to developing countries for all purposes totaled $37 billion and direct private investment exceeded $75 billion. Altogether, the flow of private funds was several times the amount of official development assistance. Projections for 1990 put the high estimates at $66 billion for official aid and $301 billion for private loans and direct investments.[9] Private joint ventures have already achieved substantial success in the operation of industrial plants, food chains, department stores, and hotels. In the future it may be possible for the transportation sector to benefit from private loan guarantees for joint business ventures in the operation of truck and bus lines, airlines, pipelines, containerized freight services, and intermodal transport companies.

Figure Seventeen / Building a road in Ethiopia. World Bank photo.

Private-sector financing could become a major factor in the improvement of Third World transport capabilities as the global dispersal of industrial and manufacturing plants continues to expose the undercapacity of ports and their road and rail connections. This lack of modern transport will impose obvious limits on the availability of good plant locations and on the productivity of overseas operations. Private firms can be expected to play a positive role in overcoming the disadvantages of inadequate transport infrastructure, and transport companies in the United States and other developed countries may extend their efforts to operate internationally.

When transportation problems are seen in their global context, it becomes obvious that the system on which the industrial nations depend is no longer limited to their own domestic facilities. The transport services affecting economic growth include the total global network that supports the world's production and its trade and travel. Developed countries could enjoy substantial long-term benefits by helping to accelerate construction of transport systems beyond their borders which will be needed to extend world markets. Like a telephone network that increases its effectiveness with increasing numbers of subscribers, the global economy will operate to maximum advantage only when the disconnected majority of humanity is plugged into the system. It is this increasingly obvious requirement that will be the critical item on the global transportation agenda in the closing years of the century.

Organizing a Global Effort

There is no focus of resposibility for assuring that world development is effectively supported by transportation services. There are international organizations, public and private, dealing with world agriculture, industry, health, housing, labor, trade, telecommunications, environment, finance, and many other international concerns. World centers of responsibility have been established for these matters, where one can gain a fairly accurate picture of how humanity is faring and what the needs and prospects for the future are. However, the transportation that has made possible these global approaches is lacking a world view. There is no inventory of transport conditions or any reliable estimates of the future volumes and types of traffic that will have to be moved. It is not known how much transport will be needed to feed a world of 6 billion people, to supply the giant cities now projected, or to support the trends in industrial production and trade.

A number of organizations participate in global efforts to further the development of transportation. They include U.N. headquarters, the U.N. Conference on Trade and Development (UNCTAD), the U.N.

Development Program (UNDP), and the U.N. regional commissions. International agencies dealing with individual methods of transport include the International Civil Aviation Organization, the International Maritime Consultative Organization, and the International Road Federation. Transportation is also an important concern of the World Bank, which comes closest to being a center of concern for the role of transportation in the world economy. But the many other responsibilities of the World Bank may preclude the more closely targeted effort that is needed to center responsibility for world transportation.

How the vacuum should be filled is a question that has lacked a satisfactory answer since the demise of the U.N. Transportation and Communications Commission, which was established in the Economic and Social Council in 1947. The commission was understandably frustrated by a mission to coordinate such diverse specialized interests as aviation, weather, postal service, and shipping. Much of the U.N.'s work in inland transportation was eventually delegated to the regional commissions on the grounds that circumstances so differed around the world that a regional approach to transportation was preferrable.

A shrinking planet has altered that perception of the problem, and a global approach to transportation has become an urgent need. A practical means of achieving such an effort might be through a network of existing specialized U.N. agencies that deal with different methods of transportion. A point somewhere in the network (for example, London, Washington, or Geneva) could function as a transportation center or secretariat. The technical capabilities of the individual agencies could be drawn upon to further Third World development and to integrate and magnify transport's economic impact. Financial assistance for the center might be provided in part by the transportation industries, while functioning of the center might be accomplished through a nongovernmental organization affiliated with the U.N. Functions of the center and network would include a continuing assessment of the state of world transport, the identification of priority needs, the design of effective international assistance programs, the analysis and dissemination of relevant information, and the establishment of a shared international agenda for transportation research.

An international transportation center would have the responsibility of furthering appropriate technical and financial assistance efforts to help close the transportation gap. It would take on the task of assuring that worldwide information and experience in the transport sector were selectively retrieved, analyzed, and made available to governments and other prospective users, through international communications networks serving ministries of transport, university transport centers, and transport industries.

A further role of the center would be to assemble teams of experienced people to participate in efforts to extend and improve the global transport system. Engineers and other experts from many countries have already participated on a broad scale in the design and execution of major transport projects and related developments. France helped build the Mexico City subway; French and Japanese engineers worked on the subway system in Seoul; and Hong Kong turned to American engineers for advice on roads and rapid transit. The deepwater port of Tema in Ghana was designed and built with the help of consultants from Greece, and Bogotá's new town proposals were planned with help from the builders of Columbia, Maryland. Australian planners supported by the U.N. helped transform Singapore, and Americans worked on the design of the Karachi metrovilles. Technical teams assembled by international financing agencies have done much to transfer available knowledge and experience. But much more needs to be accomplished in developing skills and effective organizations.

Building effective institutional arrangements and improving managerial capabilities in both the public and private sectors are essential to good project selection and implementation. Investments in transportation cannot make a maximum contribution to development without adequate organization, administration, and personnel. Aid programs need to put greater emphasis on the entire range of management problems from planning and project evaluation to hiring practices, pay scales, promotion policies, budgeting, procurement, and training. Unimpressive performance can often be attributed to such diverse factors as poor interagency communication and coordination, tax and pricing policies, and ineffective use of consultants. Overcoming such difficulties involves continuing education and training through local transportation institutes aided by the World Bank and other agencies with the necessary background and experience.

According to World Bank assessments of transportation project implementation, about three-quarters of the projects that had partial or substantial success with recommended institutional changes showed a rate of return of 10 percent or better. But where there were small or negative returns, it was more often the case that the investment programs had involved negligible efforts to upgrade institutions.[10] Cost overruns, poor traffic forecasting, and consequent design problems and financial difficulties often reflect the need for more broadly trained staff and advisors with sufficient knowledge of the local physical, cultural, and political realities as well as the economic considerations that have to be dealt with. A good start has been made at the World Bank's Economic Development Institute and through its support of training operations overseas. The cooperation of universities and other educational agencies in both the developed and less developed countries would extend the training network and increase the availability of transportation staffs with an economic development perspective.

The results that stem from institutional deficiencies can often be seen in badly operated ports, poorly maintained roads, neglected equipment, and dissatisfied shippers and travelers. In many instances the difficulties lie not only in physical inadequacies but in scheduling, marketing, and business management. Solutions often can be found in such institutional innovations as contracting with the private sector for work once performed by the government. Independent authorities and public corporations have also played a role in depoliticizing transport operations, and considerable success has followed from decentralizing transport responsibilities to give local governments wider scope for improving standards of mobility.

In the urban sector, the integration of transportation with new communities and the redevelopment of existing cities has led to a wide variety of institutional innovation. Singapore relied on a newly created government agency, the Housing and Development Board, located in the national Ministry of Planning. The Philippines relied on a private company, the Ayala Corporation, to build and operate the city of Makati, and Hong Kong centered urban development responsibilities in its public works department. Japan engaged a semi-public planned organization to act as a planning and management body that could coordinate the many different contributions of national and prefectural governments in the building of suburban cities outside Osaka, while in the Tokyo area the management of new city construction was carried out jointly by the Tokyo Metropolitan Development Corporation and the Japan Housing Public Corporation. An arrangement similar to Japan's public-private ventures in Osaka is highly successful in Curitiba, Brazil. There a public-private development corporation serves as the planning arm of the municipal government, while a development corporation with considerable state capital (but with 51 percent municipal ownership) carries out the actual work of building roads, transportation terminals, and the new industrial city.

The trend in both developed and less developed countries is to shift transportation and related development and operating responsibilities from government agencies to new combinations of public and private management or to the private sector alone. In many cases it may be preferable to take the middle route of shared public and private responsibility, avoiding the unwanted effects of government monopoly and the possibility of private-sector neglect of the public interest. A shared undertaking of both sectors appears to meld the efficiency of private business operations with a concern for broader development objectives.

A key role of a transportation center and network would be to establish priorities for research and development and to arrange for the support of research not being given adequate attention. Projects that might be on the priority list would include the development of new sources of energy, more effective methods of urban public transit, improved road-building techniques, new methods of organizing and financing transportation, and a host of other matters dealing with the safety and economy of transportation and the development of measures designed to reduce the transport burden (solar energy, new agricultural technology, and telecommunications).

Basic to the success of the transport agenda is an effective international exchange of information and expertise. With the help of low-cost telecommunications, it is possible to join with other countries in discussion, experiments, and joint research. It has become possible through information exchange to learn in advance many of the impacts of proposed financial policies, organizational arrangements, energy choices, urban design solutions, traffic engineering innovations, rapid-transit systems, and bus, truck, and airline operating strategies. Billions of dollars might be saved by using the global laboratory of experience.

In summary, world economic progress is adversely affected by the underdevelopment of Third World transport. Poor transportation is not the only cause of economic malfunctioning, but it does have an influence on almost every other aspect of the development process. Economic progress is thus being endangered by the absence of any clear responsibility for assessing the world's transportation needs and for furthering the necessary policies and programs that could narrow the transportation gap between mobile and immobile nations.

Although many international organizations are already at work to help improve world transport capabilities, there is still an insufficient focus on transport deficiencies as they relate to economic development in the Third World, and this appears to be a significant obstacle to increasing production and incomes. It is also a potential limiting factor on world trade and investment and thus a constraint on the continuing prosperity of affluent nations. A planet that is half-mobile and isolated cannot support the economic expansion demanded by a rapidly growing world still steeped in poverty. The situation calls for accelerating international assistance to help complete the global transportation network.

Seven / Global System Strategies: A Summary

An appraisal of the state of world transport and its capacity to support the anticipated growth of population and economic development generates mixed reactions. Advances in transport technology and performance have completely altered the economic, social, and political outlook for much of the world. The mobility of people and goods, and the extension of world communications, have contributed to unprecedented levels of production and income and have rendered the concept of the global village a near-reality. At the same time, the failure of the transportation revolution to touch the lives of so much of the human race has created a mobility gap that leaves 2 billion people virtually disconnected from the rest of the world. This book has explored the possibilities of extending the transport system as an essential first step toward increasing the productivity of world agriculture and industry and furthering the opportunities afforded by personal mobility. Advances in transportation promise mutual benefits for both rich countries and poor as higher levels of mobility lead to the expansion of international trade, travel, and investment, the sharing of knowledge and experience, and a lessening of the poverty that afflicts more than half the people on earth.

It took humanity several millennia to advance from its original state of immobility and poverty to the greater affluence made possible by the mechanization of transport. But once the steamship and the steam railway had speeded the processes of economic development, it was a mere eighty years to the advent of the motor age, forty more years to the age of commercial flight, and twenty years after that to the first ventures into space. The change of speed—and the speed of change—have stepped up the timetable for the global economy.

The intercontinental links are in place. But for most of the earth and its people, it is a different story. The transportation gap between rich and poor countries compels the world economy to operate under severe constraints. World production is far below capacity, incomes are minimal, and trade is stifled by the inability to gain access to land and other resources and to extend the radius of personal travel.

We live on a planet that is half-mobile and half-immobilized. Yet intercontinental ties have suddenly bound us sufficiently close together to cause the economic fortunes of all nations to be increasingly interrelated. The underlying explanation bears repeating: the world is becoming unified by a combination of technology and geography. The earth is equipped with built-in rights-of-way for intercontinental transportation—the oceans that cover two-thirds of its surface, the skies that surround it, and, beyond that, outer space. These passageways for moving people, goods, and information are provided free by nature, but they could not be used effectively until the second half of the twentieth century. It was then that the speed and capacity of ships and planes, and the availability of instantaneous communications by satellite, made it possible to take full advantage of nature's largesse. Suddenly it became feasible to interconnect the most distant parts of the planet. With this tightening web of transportation and communications came the increasing interdependence of nations and the beginnings of a world view of human progress. We had arrived on the threshold of the global economy.

The advent of the space age, the fifth stage in the development of transportation, dramatizes the obsolescence of such notions as trade restrictions, grain embargoes, communications jamming, and the denial of freedom to travel. The fifth stage calls for a precisely opposite approach to the world: greater international economic integration, the promotion of trade and travel, and the extension of personal contacts, cultural exchanges, multinational joint ventures, and cooperative interchanges in research and education.

Travel in space is altering perceptions of what might be accomplished on earth. In a more tightly compressed world, all nations have a stake in the political and economic advantages of increasing production and trade and of moving people and ideas. Looking at the earth from space makes it possible for humanity to envision common goals: nations working cooperatively to reap the benefits of access to the world's natural resources and of freedom of movement for people, goods, and information. The division of the globe between the mobile and affluent countries and the immobile and destitute ones has become an unacceptable barrier to economic progress and peaceful coexistence.

Just as exploration in space depends on complex systems of transportation, life-support, and environmental concerns, so transportation on earth has become increasingly system-oriented. The transportation future will involve intermodal systems, physically integrated systems of local, intercity, and intercontinental transport, and functional systems that integrate transportation with food delivery, manufacturing, urbanization, education, recreation, and tourism. Effective transportation strategies will have to reflect appropriate system parameters.

In the fifth stage, and by the end of the twentieth century, it will be necessary to meet the food, housing, and job needs of an additional 1 billion people. If the gross world product doubles between the mid-eighties and the year 2000, as now projected, and if half the world's people crowd into cities, the cost and complexity of meeting transportation requirements will be correspondingly greater. Food consumption, as has been noted, will need to be at least double the levels of the seventies, and industrial expansion could easily double the volume of raw materials and finished goods to be delivered. Millions more workers will commute between their homes and jobs. The explosive growth rates in many countries, added to the needs of the existing population, could make transportation a critical barrier to economic progress.

The unfinished global transportation system is a major obstacle to reducing world poverty and a barrier to higher levels of world production and consumption.

Transportation, as a means to other ends, plays a catalytic role in the performance of all sectors of the economy. Its deficiencies are felt on the overburdened routes and in the obsolete subsystems of the developed countries, as well as in the burgeoning cities and isolated rural areas of the Third World. The problems of the latter, however, are critical, and their effects are felt in the affluent nations as well as in the poor ones. Lack of mobility in low-income countries imposes limits on the access to resources, the conduct of industry, the adoption of modern farming practices, the delivery of education, and the viability of the cities. The impacts are the product of many different ingredients that contribute to economic stagnation, and transportation alone will not overcome them. But nothing can be done to address the multiple causes of poverty without first making the problems accessible and the remedies movable. Meanwhile, all of the world suffers from low levels of output, the lack of Third World purchasing power, the constraints on world trade, and the inability of surplus producers to find markets for their products.

Many different approaches will be needed to narrow the gap between the high-income countries and their isolated neighbors. The responsibility of the transportation sector is to overcome the immobility and inaccessibility that prevent other elements of the problem from being addressed.

Rich and poor countries have many transportation problems in common and should collaborate in the search for solutions.

The transportation problems of developing countries are different in magnitude from those of industrial economies, yet many of the difficulties and needed policy changes are applicable to rich and poor countries alike. Both the United States and the Third World face the need for substantial increases in transportation capacity at a time when competition for public support is intensifying. Each needs to increase transport efficiency and to introduce more effective management and new institutions if expanded requirements are to be met. Most rural areas of the world suffer from isolation, and most cities are overburdened with traffic. Financing an adequate system is a continuing challenge.

There are understandable doubts that the transport deficiencies of poor countries can be overcome in time to keep pace with the needs. But the history of transport innovation suggests that a pessimistic view is unwarranted. Just as earlier advances in technology and institutions supported economic gains in the United States and Europe, further innovations could come to the rescue of Third World countries. Major gains can also be expected from accelerating financial and technical aid to the less developed countries and from stepping up the exchange of information, the conduct of research and development, and the extension of international management of transport operations. In many instances there is sufficient similarity in the problems of rich and poor countries to warrant joint ventures in the search for new solutions. We have reached the point when all countries have a stake in the effective operation of the entire world system.

Motorization of rural road transport is essential to meeting world food requirements and needs to be accelerated in Third World countries.

The intercontinental life lines are operating at high levels of efficiency, but recent assessments of rural transportation reveal that even the transport systems serving American agriculture are in trouble. Excess road mileage, obsolete alignment, and the inadequate capacity of bridges to carry heavy equipment pose physical and financial problems for grain-producing areas. In less developed countries, the complete absence of transport frustrates the farmer. Large areas are insufficiently equipped with transport to support the growth of food for local consumption and for shipments to urban consumers. Power, seed, fertilizer, tools, schools, veterinary services, and loans are all likely to be missing in areas that lack access.

An overview of the state of world transport leads to the conclusion that local rural transport is a universally neglected part of the system and that upgrading rural mobility could have a critical impact on food security, on reducing poverty, and on creating links to the urban economy. All-weather rural transport benefits industry as well as agriculture because increases in farm incomes make possible the purchases of goods and services supplied by the cities.

The enormous investment needed to bring the rural areas of the developing world into contact with the global economy suggests two strategies. First, improvements should be limited to a specific network

of priority routes. Second, in a period in which many developing countries are heavily saddled by foreign debts, it would be counterproduc-
tive to provide more loans. What is called for is an international grant
program for road construction and maintenance to be applied to routes
serving lands that will also be the targets of other efforts to assist agriculture and rural development.

Building roads and restricting their use are contradictory policies
that have become standard operating procedure. Lagging rates of motorization and the accompanying lack of user revenues contribute to the
neglect of road maintenance and often to the abandonment of routes
built at considerable cost. It may be preferable in some circumstances to
give priority to the purchase of vehicles and to respond later to the
pressure for better roads. The United States had two and a half million
motor vehicles before 1916, when pressures exerted by the nation's
farmers (and cyclists) led to the first federal aid to help get America out
of the mud. Japan had over a million motor vehicles in the mid-fifties
when the national government first began to concern itself with Japan's
almost rudimentary road net.

Developing countries often see the motor vehicle only as a consumer
of scarce resources and a competitor of the railways. But developed
countries have demonstrated that motorized transport is also a creator
of resources and that its functions are more intimately related to the
processes of production and to the supply of services than to the under-
mining of the railways. In any event, the latter fear is now allayed by the
prospects for creating intermodal transport companies in which trucks
and rails become partners in the delivery of integrated transportation
services.

Improving the global food network in developing countries may be
viewed as potentially damaging to the export market for American
agriculture. However, world requirements will be increasing with population growth and rising incomes, and, in any case, there are limits to
the ability of developing countries to pay for imports. Increasing the
capacity of low-income countries to feed themselves will also have the
salutary effect of contributing to their ability to pay for imported manu-
factures, thus expanding the market for world industry.

*Prospects for agriculture and rural development depend on better education, and transport
deficiencies that now limit school attendance can be overcome partly by communications.*

Closely related to the outlook for modern agriculture and more rapid
rural development is the state of rural education and the ability of local
transportation to provide access to schools. In the United States, the

combination of all-weather roads and school buses permitted the assembly of students from a wide area of the countryside. As a result, it was possible to abandon small and ill-equipped schoolhouses and to substitute the large consolidated school. This led to improvement in the quality of the teaching staff, expansion of the curriculum, and better classrooms and laboratories. None of this was possible with the one-room schoolhouse with a single teacher handling all grades and all subjects.

Many of the world's developing countries have not yet arrived at the stage where either a teacher or a one-room structure is available. In India, three-fourths of the children do not attend school. A large percentage of those who do report to school have no building and attend classes in the open in good weather and bad. Teachers are in critically short supply, and there are not enough books to go around. Without transportation, it is not possible to stretch educational resources by consolidating schools.

But as demonstrated by India's experiment with satellite instructional television, an entirely new factor has been introduced into the countryside. Rural villages were afforded instruction for both adults and school-age children by means of words and pictures traveling some forty-four thousand miles from New Delhi to the satellite and back to earth in less time than it takes to move a fraction of a mile by road. For the first time it was possible to tap the accumulated knowledge of the world. A rudimentary transport connection was still needed to install power in the villages, to allow the television set to be delivered, and to put the antenna in place, but dependence on transportation was minimal. India's own satellite, *Insat,* is now delivering news, weather reports, technical assistance, and classroom exercises to remote populations that might otherwise have waited years for the transportation facilities needed to bring education within reach. The partnership of communications and transportation spells new hope for overcoming rural isolation throughout the Third World.

The network serving industry and manufacturing is deficient, and the state of Third World transport precludes the growth of rural-urban trade.

As the global dispersal of industry continues, the declining costs and rising service standards of the industrial transport network of the globe have become increasingly powerful contributors to economic growth. In the transport industry itself, the ease of international movement has encouraged shared production in the aircraft and automotive industries, and in the global restructuring of parts production and assembly plant location. Raw materials for other industries come from ever greater distances, as illustrated by coal shipments from Australia to the United

States and the movement of cement from Spain to East Coast cities. Manufacturing through international production sharing, which is dependent on the effectiveness of global transport facilities, has multiplied in value twenty times over the past twenty years. The ability of the industrial transport network to support international joint ventures is reflected in the fact that much of what is imported into the United States has a high content of U.S.-supplied ingredients that move to offshore production plants, then back to the United States in final form or for final assembly. U.S. cowhide shipped to Brazil for tanning is then shipped to Taiwan and Korea for the manufacture of baseball gloves, which in turn are shipped back to the United States to supply 95 percent of the gloves used by American players. The major leagues get their baseballs through the export of hides from the United States to Haiti, where the final product is assembled and shipped out from U.S.-owned Haitian factories.

The intercontinental links in the world transport network are performing as well for industry as they are for agriculture. But in developing countries only the major cities are well-served, and the system excludes much of the hinterland, which has untapped raw materials and lacks connections to link urban manufacturing and potential rural customers. Industry has little domestic trade other than with customers in the cities where production takes places, and it must rely on export markets to maintain an economical scale of production. As a result, all countries are hard-pressed by the competition for limited overseas demand and would gain from the opening of domestic markets in the hinterlands of developing countries which are now beyond reach largely because of the absence of transportation.

Further gains in world trade may be fostered by the expansion of international transport operations supplied through multinational corporations, joint ventures, and management contracts. Transportation equipment industries have become international, and now the operation of international transportation services has begun. United Parcel Service and Federal Express, once confined to the United States, have extended package deliveries to Europe. International air courier service is also provided by Emory, DHL, and other corporations worldwide, with arrangements for surface connections in developing countries. The next step may be an expansion of international joint ventures in the developing world which help to modernize infrastructure and services and to link international aviation and shipping with improved domestic transport systems.

Overcoming the congestion on urban links is vital to the operating efficiency of the entire global network.

The ability to move people and goods on the urban transport system heavily influences production costs and the attraction of the city to residents and businesses. Because most of the world's industrial output has its origins and destinations in the city, the congestion and disorder typical of Third World metropolitan areas have become barriers to overall economic efficiency. Despite an inordinate amount of time and money being spent to decongest the mega-cities of the developing world, it has not been possible to overcome the congestion and pollution that make the metropolis increasingly unfit for living or working.

Improved public transportation and comprehensive traffic engineering are essential. A further possibility of decongesting urban centers is to charge motorists the cost of the street capacity built to accommodate rush-hour driving. Duplicating Singapore's experience with monthly charges for drivers not in car pools could help to reduce city traffic and contribute to municipal road funds. Automatic vehicle detection, as demonstrated in Hong Kong, may make possible electronic billing of auto owners for their specific travels on the street system and might help to achieve more equitable allocation of street space and a fairer assessment of costs.

The advantages of making better use of existing systems through traffic engineering, improved public transit, and pricing policies, have not been widely realized, however, nor have urban commuters who depend on public carriers been given the help that could come from all-transit streets, larger bus fleets, and better taxi and van service.

The conclusion has been reached, nevertheless, that neither low-cost traffic and pricing policies nor high-cost expressway and rapid-transit solutions is likely to overcome the constraints on the transport system imposed by the density and disorder of unplanned cities. Successful efforts to accommodate urban growth in many parts of the world have focused instead on urban design: building better planned living and working environments in the outlying urban fringes and simultaneously redeveloping the older parts of the city.

Lessons learned from growth policies in Europe, Asia, and Latin America indicate the possibilities of using transportation to help disperse population and employment in preplanned partially self-contained communities removed from central cities. Road and rail transport serves the more extensive urban regions that result, and transport is supplemented by low-cost telecommunications. It is also possible to reduce commuter traffic by making it feasible for some types of jobs and economic activities to be located closer to affordable housing.

The success of city-building strategies in Sweden, England, and Japan are among the examples that suggest more consciously designed dispersal as the logical antidote for the overconcentrations resulting from earlier dependence mainly on rail and water transport, compounded by the lack of good local circulation. Air transport, motorization, and means of communication now foster greater dispersal and can lead to more transport-conserving urban designs. A key to such solutions is advance land acquisition for preplanned communities that can absorb new growth in a more decentralized environment. Increased land values resulting from urban growth may then be the source of revenues to help pay for urban services. Rights of way for transportation to serve the multiple centers of the regional city can also be paid for this way.

Multicentered regional cities modeled after Stockholm, Hong Kong, Singapore, and new communities in Japan and France could help free the transportation system of the congestion that now threatens cities such as Mexico City, Rio de Janeiro, São Paulo, Lagos, Manila, and Bangkok. A rapidly urbanizing world needs to use more than the 1 or 2 percent of the earth's surface now being dedicated to cities.

Transportation and urban design solutions already tested in a number of countries could benefit cities in the United States and elsewhere. The United States in particular needs to launch an effective long-term program to eliminate its urban slums and to bring about a more orderly growth of its suburbs and exurbs. American inner cities confront an awesome combination of poor housing, inadequate services, unemployment, untrained workers, and bad environment. Although it is hardly possible to compare the problems of the United States with those that were overcome by tiny Singapore, the differences in geography, politics, and scale do not lessen the relevance of what Singapore did to train, employ, and house its poor.

Singapore put investments in shelter, services, and environment ahead of investments in transportation, yet it made transportation the framework around which redevelopment took place. Limited-access roadways provided transport to the new suburbs, and the regional city combined traffic engineering with congestion-pricing policies to reduce the pressures of automobile travel. It also combined housing, jobs, schools, and shops in clustered developments to help stem the tide of traffic. Landscaped highways throughout the island proclaim the dual role of transportation in the urban setting: to move the traffic but also to help create a satisfying environment. Singapore adopted transport strategies designed to help the poor, and in the process it became rich.

Networks for domestic and international travel and tourism contribute to economic development and need to be extended.

One distinction between rich and poor countries is the size of the travel gap. At the beginning of the twentieth century, the average U.S. citizen was hardly more mobile than people living in the isolation of low-income developing countries today. The travel figure was not much more than a mile a day. Now, thanks to the automobile and the airplane, the average American travels some twelve thousand miles a year, compared to about four hundred miles in 1900—about the same figure for poor countries in 1985. The purpose of travel has also been altered. The journey to work, which once accounted for nearly all passenger movement in the United States, has declined in relative importance, and two-thirds of today's travel is for social and recreational purposes and other personal trips.

Vacationing and tourism are creating what may soon become the world's largest industry. International tourism has reached a level of several hundred million persons a year. The impacts of tourism include education in history, geography, and culture, and the opportunity for achieving greater international understanding and good will. Also important are foreign-exchange receipts, which in some developing countries already exceed what is earned from the major crop or the principal industry. Extending the tourist network provides an added impetus for building better world systems of transportation and communications, along with the hotels and other facilities that compose the total system of global travel. The natural scenery and cultural wealth of the developing world indicate the potential benefits of furthering vacation travel and reaping the economic returns from tourism. Realizing the benefits will necessitate large investments to assure the rail, highway, and air services that the travel industry requires.

Passenger mobility may be as important or more important to economic development than the movement of freight. But systems of passenger mobility are grossly inadequate for the day-to-day travels of those who live in developing countries. The barrier to education, formal and informal, is an example. Travel to a school or to the nearest town may be impossible on any regular basis, which restricts activities and is a major source of the knowledge gap. Immobility makes it impossible to share in the benefits conferred by the long history of human experience. The emphasis on freight movement denies the central importance of personal mobility in the conduct of business and farming, in the search for jobs, and in the use of community services.

If the great majority of the earth's people are to be linked to the outside world, the travel networks needed may be long in coming, and immediate hope may lie instead in the uses of telecommunications. Substituting communications for transportation makes it possible to provide needed help in farming practices, personal hygiene, nutrition, animal husbandry, road-building, irrigation works, marketing, and classroom instruction. The establishment of telephone, television, and other communications links could help developing countries anticipate by many years the benefits that would otherwise be realized only after completion of costly transportation networks.

Just as the air age stepped up the timetable for the global economy, telecommunications has hastened the need to deliver to the local economy the tools, materials, and comforts that television reveals to be available elsewhere. The dissemination of information on television screens calls for physical access to carry out the kinds of advice that are telecast. Better agricultural practices require the delivery of fertilizer, and better health calls for clean water and sanitation facilities. These require transportation to bring materials and equipment to the village. Growing produce for sale to increase farm income requires reliable transportation to regulated markets. Better education requires that teachers and students get to school. The information age can be expected to increase the demands for financial support and technology transfer to help the millions newly exposed to the outside world.

The expanding global economy calls for more effective strategies for financing the system.

Many developing countries burdened with debt and critically short of public funds can expect that official development assistance for transportation will be more difficult to come by in the future. One alternative will be greater amounts of private capital. Another is the introduction of user charges and rate policies that increase self-support in the transport sector. A third is the levying of an international user charge on world trade and travel which could build a fund to support higher levels of concessional financing by the World Bank and regional banking institutions. Still another prospect is the extension into developing countries of transport services operated by international corporations.

Already there is a move toward increased private financing. The private sector is providing urban travel facilities by jitneys and vans in the cities of relatively low-income countries. American cities are following a similar pattern as businesses and service organizations operate their own paratransit fleets to substitute for unsatisfactory public transport. Toll finance, which began on a large scale in Europe, is now relied upon to a greater extent in the United States and Japan. It may be a solution for developing countries, for toll roads in several Asian and Latin American countries demonstrate the feasibility of this approach to paying part of the bill for high-cost facilities.

Direct investment by private firms in their own foreign subsidiaries or in partnership with foreign companies is a significant source of capital. It also supplies valuable technical assistance and expands the supply of managerial talent. However, most private funds are made available only to the more developed countries, where economic and political conditions are favorable. From 1980 through 1983, the flow of direct capital investment funds to developed countries totaled some $31 billion, while developing countries received only $13 billion and most of that was given to a few middle-income recipients, such as Brazil, Mexico, Malaysia, and Singapore. Direct investment was not of major help to low-income countries.

The prospects for the long term are more positive, as the World Bank's International Finance Corporation continues to aid the flow of international investment and as investment guarantees hold the promise of reducing the risk of noncommercial losses. Private capital for transportation was once an important contributor to the now developed countries, and it might be influential once again.

But the problem of accelerating the construction and maintenance of the publicly provided infrastructure remains, and especially the financing of roads. The deficiency in road access is an underlying factor in underdevelopment, and its contribution to isolation can be measured by the variations in mileage relative to land area. In the United States there is approximately one mile of road per square mile of territory, and in Europe there is slightly more than one mile per square mile. But Latin America has five times as many square miles of land as it has miles of road. The ratio is nearly four to one in Asia and twenty to one in Africa. Taking into account the three and a half million square miles of African desert, the ratio is still sixteen to one.

The physical magnitude of the road-building task and the financial support that would be needed to maintain adequate global systems are not unlike the tasks that faced the United States in an earlier period. The concept of a transfer of capital from wealthier areas in the form of grants to poorer parts of the country contributed to building one million miles of roads in twenty years. User taxes levied by the states helped to cover part of the cost. The development of trade and travel connections in the now inaccessible rural areas of the globe promises political and economic benefits not unlike those that followed from opening the North American continent. The prospects have suggested grants instead of loans, financed by a modest charge for the use of international trade and travel routes that benefit from the free rights of way provided by nature. Such a levy could create a continuing and predictable source of funds, which the World Bank could make available on a near-grant basis through the IDA. The transportation needed for an expanding global economy calls for a global commitment to help pay the early development costs.

Transportation problems can be resolved by nontransportation solutions.

The solution of the world's transportation problems calls for outlays and undertakings far beyond the capacity available to deal with them. But lately it has become apparent that remedies lie not simply in supplying more facilities but in an entirely different direction—in nontransportation solutions that alter the nature of the task to be accomplished. In cities, it was found that urban design might be part of the answer to congestion rather than simply building more highways and railways. In agriculture, biotechnology and plant genetics could create more convenient locations for growing food, and lessen the need for transporting commercial fertilizers. The movement of water and sewage by systems of underground pipes reduces the daily chores of many millions who would otherwise be engaged in transporting water from the wells and standpipes, or who would be carting off the city's human wastes. In the energy sector, great tonnages of solid fuel no longer need to be moved, as their place is taken by the transmission of electricity by wire, by the production of nuclear power, or by the use of solar energy delivered by nature.

Many other examples are surfacing around the world. The lumber industry moves its sawmills close to sources of timber to lessen the transportation of waste materials. Food processors do the same thing—extracting the juices from fruit and leaving the residue behind. Home computers have begun to establish the convenience and efficiency of home offices that require less frequent commuting. Teleconferencing, which provides two-way interactive voice and picture communication, is permitting more frequent get-togethers of company staffs, who once spent much time and money converging at airport hotels to discuss matters that videoconferences could handle more expeditiously. Electronic mail promises to remove considerable tonnages of paper from the daily deliveries of the postal service.

The declining costs and increasing performance of communications and computers may render obsolete much of the expensive and time-consuming travel for business. Many firms have already discovered that bringing people into the main office for consultation is not only a high-cost budget item but takes excessive company time as well. As communications costs fall more sharply with the expansion of satellite and fiber optic networks, the ease and economy of videoconferencing could completely alter business practices and travel budgets. Although travel is by no means rendered superfluous, telecommunications could increase the frequency of group meetings and the amount of personal contact and information-sharing in the businesses of the future.

These prospects on the demand side, and the technical and institutional innovations that are capable of improving the supply of transportation, focus attention on the potentials of research and development and on the exchange of ideas and experience. The fifth stage in the conquest of time and distance—the space age—holds the promise of an effective international collaboration that will help to complete the unfinished transportation system of the earth.

Because nations confront urgent transportation problems in common and will find mutual benefits in their solution, there is a strong case for a greater international commitment aimed at furthering the globe's transport capabilities.

The effort to introduce new institutions and innovative technology to help low-income countries coincides with a growing need in affluent societies to discover ways of dealing with problems of increasing congestion, rising costs, diminishing public support, and outmoded policies and institutions. The community of interests suggests cooperative international action in education and training, research and development, exchange of people and ideas, and the building and operation of facilities.

Where does responsibility lie for encouraging collaborative international efforts in the transport sector? The question is ironic, because most other economic sectors have already established world centers of responsibility in response to the changes brought about by advances in transportation. But transportation shows no similar efforts to provide a world view and to assure its effective role in economic development. Why this should be so can be attributed in part to the divisions of the transportation field into technological compartments, which in turn are reflected in the many international organizations dealing with separate parts of the subject. They are both numerous and technically competent, but their total impact on world development would be magnified if their competence were to be focused as well on comprehensive transportation strategies aimed at economic development.

That neither international organizations, individual nations, nor the private sector has embraced the cause of viewing transportation as a whole in relation to development is not difficult to understand. In a recent survey for the government of Canada, opinions were gathered on whether there was need for a world transportation center. Many of those interviewed were troubled by the idea of adding still another transportation agency to those already existing in the U.N., in Europe, and elsewhere. More dubious, it seems, was whether such a center would have any productive function beyond what existing agencies are already accomplishing.

The misgivings can be appreciated. The world is already served by the work of agencies such as the International Civil Aviation Organization, the World Bank, the European Economic Community, the U.N.'s headquarters offices and its regional commissions. But what is lacking is a focus on the critical transportation problems of the developing world. There needs to be a commitment to speeding the process of connecting the immobilized half of the planet to the rest of the world. Immobility and isolation have become an obstacle not only to the well-being of poor countries but to the long-term prosperity of the global economy. The Canadian study made jointly by Toronto and York universities came to what seems the logical conclusion: there is need for a central focus, preferably somewhere within an existing organization, to assume the responsibility for addressing the transportation problems of developing countries as they relate to economic growth.[1]

Progress toward completing a basic network of transportation for the earth requires a continuing assessment of what is needed, how best to meet the needs, what costs are involved, and what institutional changes and other actions are called for to bring about the desired results. A critical element is the upgrading of human resources through the training of engineers, managers, and transport planners and operators. Transportation institutes and university transportation centers will need to be expanded in both developed and developing countries for education and research aimed at creating a new generation of leaders concerned with the relation of mobility to development. Financial support for development-oriented transport centers could be provided in part by the transportation industries that have so large a stake in an expanded global system.

Restricted levels of international trade and of global economic activity are rooted in the mismatch between the economic vitality of the rich and mobile nations and the relative stagnation of the isolated and immobile ones.

Advances in intercontinental transport and communications have made it possible to expand the radius of the market to global dimensions. But the failure of the transport revolution to affect a large part of humanity has meant that the new mobility has had only partial impact. Without further extension of the transport system, much of the world has limited capacity to produce and consume and is largely excluded from trading. The imbalance in international transactions stems in part from the imbalance in economic development.

Reducing the lag in Third World development is a complex and long-term problem, which calls for overcoming isolation in order to supply capital, technology, education, and the necessary innovations in policy, organization, and management. The importance of transportation lies in its ability to deliver the many other ingredients of economic progress. But initial transport costs are high, and the recommended long-term solution of collecting a world user charge to finance the basic system cannot satisfy immediate needs. Some type of emergency financing is called for.

A useful precedent may be the U.S. initiative to accelerate European recovery in the late 1940s, when close to $20 billion was made available over a four-year period, mostly in grants, to stimulate recovery in postwar Western Europe. If history were to be repeated in a different context, the OECD countries might now join to supply emergency grants to finance the infrastructure needed for the economic takeoff of Third World countries. Poor nations overburdened with debt and the victims of a general economic slowdown are no less a threat to the future of the world economy than the devastation suffered by postwar Europe. Even greater economic and political benefits than those of the Marshall Plan might follow from a comparable effort to narrow the gap between rich countries and poor ones.

In summary, the current stage in the evolution of transportation introduces the possibility that global mobility can bring about a new era of international collaboration aimed at greater efficiency and equity in the use of the world's resources. The new mobility makes possible a common vision: a world of growing interdependence working cooperatively to expand the global economy, to release more of the world's material wealth, and to provide the logistical systems needed to hasten the escape from hunger and poverty. The division of the world between the mobile and the immobile nations has become a barrier to human progress which compels an international rescue mission. Under these circumstances, transportation policy makers and the transportation industries are offered an exceptional challenge and opportunity. By helping to overcome the immobility and isolation that contribute to economic underachievement, they can set the stage for increased world output, expanded international trade, higher per capita incomes, and improved levels of living for the majority of humankind. As the transportation tasks that lie ahead continue to assume global dimensions, those involved in the age-old struggle to overcome time and distance are suddenly called upon to serve two countries—their own and the planet earth.[2]

Notes

One / A Global Overview

1. The principal source of world transportation data is the *U.N. Statistical Yearbook*, published annually by the United Nations, New York. Supplementary sources include the International Road Federation's *World Road Statistics*, Washington, D.C., and *Motor Vehicle Facts and Figures,* published annually by the Motor Vehicle Manufacturers Association, Detroit. Country population and economic data are found in the *World Development Report,* published annually by the World Bank, Washington, D.C.

2. See C. Fred Bergsten, Thomas Horst, and Theodore H. Moran, *American Multinationals and American Interests* (Washington, D.C.: Brookings Institution, 1978), pp. 10, 355. See also Bergsten in *Transatlantic Perspectives* (Washington, D.C.: German Marshall Fund, February 1982), p. 1.

3. Motor Vehicle Manufacturers Association, *Facts and Figures '85* (Detroit, 1985), pp. 31–35.

4. Mihajlo Mesarovic and Eduard Pestel, *Mankind at the Turning Point: The Second Report to the Club of Rome* (New York: E. P. Dutton, 1976), p. 76.

5. World Bank, *Energy in the Developing Countries* (Washington, D.C., August 1980), pp. 3–5.

6. Tokyo Metropolitan Government, "Official Report of the Conference of World's Great Cities" (Tokyo, 1972), p. 22.

7. The Pacific Area Conference of Municipalities (PACOM), Tapei, 1974.

Two / Mobility and World Food Supplies

1. U.S. Department of Agriculture, *1983 Handbook of Agricultural Charts* (Washington, D.C., 1983), no. 619, p. 65.

2. Food and Agricultural Organization of the United Nations, *Annual Report* (Rome, 1984), 38:269.

3. U.S. Council on Environmental Quality and the Department of State, *The Global 2000 Report to the President* (Washington, D.C., 1980), 2:77, 99.

4. Port of New York and New Jersey Authority, "Foreign Trade," 1980, p. 17.

5. R. D. Hunt, *Fruit and Vegetable Exports from the Mediterranean Area to the EEC,* Staff Working Paper No. 321 (Washington, D.C.: World Bank, March 1979).

6. Motor Vehicle Manufacturers Association, "Lifelines" (Detroit, n.d.), pp. 6–18.

7. U.S. Department of Transportation, Federal Railroad Administration, "Railroad Freight Traffic Flows, 1990" (Washington, D.C., December 1980).

8. Roland W. Merwin, "Sulfur," in *Mineral Facts and Problems* (Washington, D.C.: Government Printing Office, 1976), p. 1057.

9. C. Phillip Baumer and Eldo Schornhorst, "Local Rural Roads and Bridges:

Current and Future Problems and Alternatives," in *Research Record 898* (Washington, D.C.: Transportation Research Board, National Research Council, 1983).

10. Balu Bumb, *A Survey of the Fertilizer Sector in India,* Staff Working Paper No. 331 (Washington, D.C.: World Bank, June 1979), p. 9.

11. Ibid., pp. 65–66.

12. World Bank, "The Milk Revolution in India," in *World Development Report 1982* (Washington, D.C., 1983), box 7.2, p. 83.

13. International Road Federation, *World Highways* (Washington, D.C., October 1982), 23, no. 8, p. 3.

14. Government of India, "Transport and Communications," in *Indian Planning Commission, Draft Outline, Sixth Five-Year Plan* (New Delhi, 1978), p. 209.

15. World Bank, "Food Security in Rural China," in *World Development Report 1982* (Washington, D.C., 1983), box 7.4, p. 88.

16. A. Doak Barnett, *China and the World Food System* (Washington, D.C.: Overseas Development Council, 1979).

17. Fred H. Sanderson and Shyamal Roy, *Foods Trends and Prospects in India* (Washington, D.C.: Brookings Institution, 1979), p. 166.

18. Europa Publications, *The Europa Year Book, 1981* (London, 1981), 2:120.

19. World Bank, *Agriculture Land Settlement,* Issues Paper (Washington, D.C., January 1978), pp. 20–21.

20. World Bank, *The Road Maintenance Problem and International Assistance* (Washington, D.C., December 1981), pp. 4, 18.

21. World Bank, *Annual Report, 1979* (Washington, D.C., 1979), p. 39.

22. Sung Hwan Ban, "The New Community Movement," in *Essays on the Korean Economy,* ed. Chuk Kyo Kim, Industrial and Social Development Issues (Seoul: Korea Development Institute, 1978), 2:206.

23. Robert J. Saunders, Jeremy J. Warford, and Bjorn Wellenius, *Telecommunications and Economic Development* (Baltimore: Johns Hopkins University Press, 1983).

Three / Supporting Industrial Development

1. World Bank, *Survey of World Railways* (Washington, D.C., 1980), p. 16.

2. U.S. transport data from Transportation Policy Associates, *Transportation in America* (Washington, D.C., November 1985, and annual editions).

3. U.S. Department of Commerce, *U.S. Industrial Outlook* (Washington, D.C., 1984, and annual editions).

4. Brinton C. Brown, "Cement," in U.S. Bureau of Mines, *Mineral Facts and Problems* (Washington, D.C., 1975), p. 205.

5. *AirCargo World* 73, no. 2 (February 1983): 16–33.

6. World Bank, *World Development Report* (Washington, D.C., 1981), p. 138, and ibid., 1985, table 3, p. 178.

7. World Bank, *Energy in the Developing Countries* (Washington, D.C., August 1980), p. 2.

8. World Bank, *Thailand,* Country Study (Washington, D.C., March 1980), p. 117.

9. Indian data are from Indian Planning Commission, *Sixth Plan Outline,*

1983–88 (New Delhi, 1982). See also International Roads Federation, *World Highways* 25, no. 1 (January 1984): 2.

10. See World Bank, *China: The Economy, Statistical System and Basic Data,* Country Study (Washington, D.C., 1983), 2:129–35.

11. Data on the landlocked countries' transport problems are from the United Nations Commission on Trade and Development, Geneva.

Four / Cities in the Global Network

1. World Bank, "National Urbanization Policies in Developing Countries," Working Paper No. 347 (Washington, D.C., 1979).

2. For a discussion of urban transport management and pricing policies, see my earlier books *The Accessible City* and *Transportation for Cities* (Washington, D.C.: Brookings Institution, 1972 and 1976, respectively).

3. See Organization for Economic Cooperation and Development, "Better Towns with Less Traffic" (Paris, April 1975).

4. Wilfred Owen, "Automobiles and Cities: Strategies for Developing Countries," in *The Automobile and the Environment: An International Perspective,* ed. Ralph Gakenheimer (Cambridge, Mass.: MIT Press, 1978).

5. Data are based on Boris S. Pushkarev and Jeffrey M. Zupan, *Public Transportation and Land Use Policy* (Bloomington: Indiana University Press, 1977), p. 29.

6. Unpublished data are from David Bayliss, Chief Planner (Transportation), Greater London Council, England, 1981.

7. Harvey Cox, *The Secular City* (New York: MacMillan Press, 1966), p. 171.

8. The original book, *A Peaceful Path to Real Reform,* was published in 1898. It was revised in 1902 under the title *Garden Cities of Tomorrow* (Cambridge, Mass.: MIT Press, 1965).

9. Government of Japan, National Land Agency, "An Outline of the Third Basic Development Plan for the National Region of Japan" (Tokyo, 1977), p. 3.

10. *Nihon Keizai Shimbun,* Tokyo (27 July 1982): 11.

11. Hayo Shiina, "Transport Planning for Tsukuba New Town," *The Wheel Extended* (Spring 1976): 10–19.

12. Public Works Department of Hong Kong, *Hong Kong's New Towns: Sha Tin* (Hong Kong, 1975).

13. Data are from Chung-Hayun Ro, "Rural-Urban Migration: Alternative Responses," prepared for HABITAT Foreign Workshop (Vancouver, 1 June 1976).

14. Peter L. Watson and Edward P. Holland, "Congestion Pricing—The Example of Singapore," *Finance and Development* 13, no. 1 (March 1976): 22.

15. *El Salitre: A City in the City.* Prepared by the American City Corporation (Bogotá: Department of National Planning, Colombia, 1974).

16. See Lauchlin Currie, *Taming the Metropolis: A Design for Urban Growth* (London: Pergamon Press, in cooperation with the United Nations, 1976), p. 127.

17. Government of Pakistan, *Karachi Development Plan, 1974–1985* (Karachi, August 1974). See also Government of Pakistan, *Low-income Settlement in Karachi,* Final Report, National Pilot Project No. 3 (Karachi, January 1977).

18. The American City Corporation, *The Greater Hartford Process,* 1972. For a

further account of the Hartford Process, see Harvey S. Perloff et al., *Modernizing the Central City: New Towns in Town and Beyond* (Cambridge, Mass.: Ballinger Publishing Co., 1975), chap. 9.

19. René Dubos, *So Human an Animal* (New York: Charles Scribner, 1968), p. 180.

Five / Personal Mobility and Opportunity

1. Pierre Teilhard de Chardin, *The Phenomenon of Man* (New York: Harper and Brothers, 1959), p. 240.

2. *Tourism Marketing and Management Issues,* ed. Donald E. Hawkins et al. (Washington, D.C.: George Washington University Press, 1980).

3. U.S. Bureau of the Census, *Statistical Abstract of the United States* (Washington, D.C.: Government Printing Office, 1982), p. 32.

4. Zafer Ecevit and K. C. Zachariah, "International Labor Migration," *Finance and Development* (Washington, D.C.: International Monetary Fund and World Bank, December 1978): 32–37.

5. William G. Carr, "Education," in J. Federic Dewhurst and associates, *America's Needs and Resources* (New York: Twentieth Century Fund, 1947), p. 301.

6. U.S. Bureau of the Census, *Statistical Abstract of the United States* (Washington, D.C., 1981), p. 150.

7. U.S. Bureau of the Census, *Travel during 1977, 1978* (Washington, D.C.: Government Printing Office, 1979), p. 5.

8. *World Road Statistics,* 1980 ed. (Detroit: International Road Federation, 1980), pp. 12–19.

9. Data based on Transport Canada, *Passenger and Goods Transportation: An International Comparison, 1900–1977* (Ottawa, May 1981), p. 35.

10. National Transportation Policy Study Commission, *National Transportation Policies through the Year 2000* (Washington, D.C., June 1979), pp. 231–32.

11. Christopher Willoughby, "Transportation Research and the Developing Countries" (Paper delivered at the International Meeting on Transportation Research, Amalfi, Italy, 11–14 November 1981).

12. Asian Development Bank, *Regional Study of the Impact of the Energy Situation on Transport Development* (Manila, 1983), appendix 2.

13. John Kenneth Galbraith, *Economics, Peace, and Laughter* (Boston: Houghton Mifflin, 1971), p. 208.

Six / Marshaling the Necessary Resources

1. Congressional Budget Office, *Public Works Infrastructure: Policy Considerations for the 1980's* (Washington, D.C., April 1983), pp. 27–29.

2. Ralph J. Watkins and associates, *Report on the Kobe-Nagoya Expressway* (Tokyo: Ministry of Construction, 1956).

3. Inter-American Development Bank, *Annual Report, 1981* (Washington, D.C., 1981), p. 33.

4. World Bank, *Annual Report, 1986* (Washington, D.C., 1986), p. 143.

5. Organization for Economic Cooperation and Development, *World Economic Interdependence and the Evolving North-South Relationship* (Paris, 1983), p. 70.

6. Willy Brandt and Anthony Sampson, eds., *North-South: A Program for Survival* (*The Brandt Report*) (Cambridge, Mass.: MIT Press, 1980), p. 291.

7. Eleanor E. Steinberg and Joseph A. Yeager, with Gerard M. Brannon, *New Means of Financing International Needs* (Washington, D.C.: Brookings Institution, 1978), p. 214.

8. Bruce MacLaury, "Foreword," in ibid.

9. World Bank, *World Development Report, 1981* (Washington, D.C., 1981), p. 13.

10. World Bank, *Ninth Annual Review of Profit Performance and Audit Results* (Washington, D.C., 1983), p. 23.

Seven / Global Systems Strategy: A Summary

1. A. Cubukgil, Z. J. Haritas, and R. M. Soberman, *Assessment of the Need for a World Transport Research Center* (Toronto: York University and the University of Toronto, 1985).

2. Barbara Ward and René Dubos, *Only One Earth* (New York: Ballantine Books, 1972), p. xx.

Select Bibliography

Adler, Hans A. *Economic Appraisal of Transport Projects.* Baltimore: Johns Hopkins University Press, 1987.

Baum, Warren C., and Stokes M. Tolbert. *Investing in Development: Lessons from World Bank Experience.* New York: Oxford University Press, 1985.

Brown, Lester R. *World without Borders.* New York: Random House, 1972.

Farris, Martin T., and Paul T. McElhiney. *Modern Transportation: Selected Readings.* Houghton-Mifflin Co., 1973.

Karen, Ruth, ed. *Toward the Year 2000.* New York: William Morrow and Co., 1985.

Laszlo, Ervin. *A Strategy for the Future: The Systems Approach to World Order.* New York: Braziller, 1974.

Mahoney, John J. *Intermodal Freight Transportation.* Westport, Conn.: Eno Foundation for Transportation, 1985.

Meyer, John R., and José A. Gómez Ibáñez. *Autos, Transit, and Cities.* Cambridge, Mass.: Harvard University Press, 1981.

National Research Council. *Outlook for Science and Technology.* San Francisco: W. H. Freeman and Co., 1982.

Rostow, W. W. *The World Economy: History and Prospect.* Austin: University of Texas Press, 1978.

Scott, Roy V. *Railroad Development Programs in the Twentieth Century.* Ames: Iowa State University Press, 1985.

Sewell, John W., et al. *The United States and World Development: Agenda 1980.* Washington, D.C.: Praeger, 1980.

Sundquist, James L. *Dispersing Population: What America Can Learn from Europe.* Washington, D.C.: Brookings Institution, 1975.

Toffler, Alvin. *The Third Wave.* New York: William Morrow and Co., 1980.

U.S. Department of Commerce, International Trade Administration. *1986 U.S. Industrial Outlook.* Washington, D.C., 1986.

Ward, Barbara. *The Home of Man.* New York: W. W. Norton and Co., 1976.

Wilson, George W., et al. *The Impact of Highway Investment on Development.* Washington, D.C.: Brookings Institution, 1966.

Index

Wilfred Owen is a guest scholar at the Brookings Institution and is a former senior fellow and director of its transportation programs. He is the author of *The Accessible City, Strategy for Mobility, Distance and Development*, and other books.

Transportation and World Development

Designed by Chris L. Smith
Composed by Professional Book Compositors, Inc., in Bembo text and display
Printed by Thomson-Shore, Inc., on 50-lb. Warren's Olde Style